Soul Listening

with

Beth

SECOND BOOK OF THE
SOUL LISTENING TRILOGY
AVAILABLE FROM AMAZON

Soul Listening
Copyright 2012 Beth

All rights reserved. No part of this publication may be reproduced or transmitted in any form or by any means, electronic or mechanical, including photo-copying, recording or any information storage or retrieval system, without either prior permission in writing from the publisher or a licence permitting restricted copying.

Front cover background image:
Star Forming Region LH 95 in the Large Magellanic Cloud
NASA, ESA, and The Hubble Heritage (STScI/AURA)-ESA/Hubble Collaboration
HST/ACS STScl-PRC06-55

Typeset in Times New Roman 10pt

ISBN 978 0 9572745 0 1

Published by R.A. Associates 2012
Designed and printed in the UK
mail@whitefeather.org.uk

dedicated to
Rodney McLeod

Contents

Episode One
In search of my Soul

Episode Two
Going with Soul

Episode Three
Soul Listening

Episode One
In search of my Soul

I thought that my way now was to write a book about my experiences; I felt quite confident about that. It would have to have purpose wouldn't it, but I had identified that hadn't I? It would have to have reason wouldn't it, but I knew that didn't I?

So here I am confronted by the empty screen of this technological wizardry, this humming powerhouse of machinery; confronted once again by the limitations of my being. It is numbing, my mind clogs, fogs. Where to find those magic words, those spellbinding ideas that flash about the mind when I'm up to my elbows in washing-up water or round the bend with the Harpic?

I question; "what am I doing now, here, tapping my one fingered way around this keyboard?" I am no typist, my computing skills have only just ventured out. Last month when my dusting created life within this grey plastic contraption, my best resort was to phone a family member at work to confess the deed, with the hope of reassurance that the pictures and noises could be left in place until someone 'with the knowledge' came home.

I question again, as the words I want to share pour into my head to be lost in the slowness of my tapping. This machine is a challenge, no doubt about that. I don't much care for many modern ways. I miss the anticipation of slitting the envelope that reveals that old fashioned delight, a hand written letter. These regimental shapes have no SOUL.

Well that came as a surprise. I was hardly aware that I had got beyond my opening gambit. Muttering along with my strangled thoughts and squeezed out words, mutterings to remind myself of the accomplished speed of my longhand skills, reminders of the, as new, dictaphone in its case in the drawer; muttering admonishments and always those questions. Then there it sat before me, SOUL emblazoned in capitals, suddenly, there, staring out at me. The word slipped from my fingertips on to the screen.

I will cease the reasoning, the puzzling, cease the justifications for this writing and simply get on with it. Soul is the reason I'm sitting here, Soul is the purpose of my tome. Soul made itself known to me and Soul won't let go, so please come with me as I go with Soul to share with you the most extraordinary and exciting, frightening yet enlightening times of my life.

In search of my Soul

Soul was handed to me on a plate, more precisely in a pack of cards. Let me explain, but first of all on the theme of explanation I want to draw your attention to something which will probably be a recurring ploy of mine throughout this book; that is the introduction of dictionary definitions for important words. This is not to foster the belief that I am indeed the "bossy old school ma'am" I have, not so lovingly, been called during a time in my life that I prefer to forget; although I know that it will inevitably nose its way into these pages alongside other truly forgettable times which come together to make up the journey from there to here.

I want to share my journey with you. That is an acknowledgement not easily made. You see, I feel myself to be so very ordinary, not the sort of person you would notice on the street, definitely invisible in a crowd, very much the acclaimed 'speck of human anonymity', mere dust in the great cosmos, and yet, and yet, I want to be heard by you. I want you to understand; so those parts that read like a dictionary are offered for the purpose of clarity and understanding.

As the side-roads of my journey link themselves into the highway of this tale you will easily come to see how my need to have you understand my words stems from my need to understand the particular world that has been my place of learning. This desire to understand, to make sense of, has been a spur and a bugbear, and this thread will weave its way in and out of my story. By the time we reach the here and now together, you will know me: I hope some may know themselves better as a result of sharing my pitfalls and occasional triumphs. If you laugh once along the way I will be happy and if you discover your Soul I'll be over the moon!

To the dictionary, SOUL *spiritual or immaterial part of man, held to survive death.* Back to that book again, SPIRITUAL .... and there before me is a paragraph of attempts to define spiritual. Well that is all very familiar to me having spent twenty and more years on the so called 'spiritual pathway' rubbing shoulders with many and varied seekers of spirituality, spiritual enlightenment, spiritual growth, indeed all and every venture under the many and varied interpretations of that word spiritual.

Still so near to the beginning of this book and I find myself up against the very thing that I set out to avoid, misunderstandings. The dictionary again? I think so. Immaterial strikes a friendly chord in my being. IMMATERIAL *not material, incorporeal,* oh no, are we off again? INCORPOREAL *not composed of matter.* I can breathe a sigh of relief; that says it all for me. Simply, the Soul is not matter.

For a while there I was beginning to feel that fog of uncertainty again. What I see as a simple issue looked in danger of being swirled into the misty clouds of indefiniteness, I could almost feel myself being sucked to the very edge of the religious debate. Easily done, the words spiritual and soul to me have been synonymous with religion, maybe to you too? No-one would describe me as a religious person, the church going, the dogma and ceremony, no; "God-bothering" my old farming neighbour used to call that. But I do have beliefs and I do have faith and now seems the appropriate time to spell those out to you. We all know where we stand then.

My faith comes from my belief that there is something that unites us all; that threads its way through every known and unknown atom of the cosmos. That something is the energy of Unconditional Love. Perhaps you read that as good, perhaps you shorten that good to god. It's all the same difference. In my life, in my work, and here in my book it's Unconditional Love, of which you are going to hear much, much more before I'm through with this.

Soul, the part of man that is not matter. Did I hear some-one then, if it is not matter it doesn't exist? Well that may be your understanding, your truth, but it is no longer mine. With the understanding between us that not so long ago, despite years of believed spiritual searching, I didn't know that I was the proud owner of a Soul; I am going to tell you how my own Soul and the universal or cosmic Soul miraculously made my acquaintance. Incidentally, COSMIC *of the universe or cosmos*, COSMOS (and out of the proposals here I select for my purpose) *sum-total of experience*. I experience myself becoming so easily side-tracked, thumbing round the pages, looking at the multitude of themes that just one word can express. I realise that the understanding of any word is very much ones own, uniquely born of the experiences of each one of us. Can we then satisfactorily communicate using the spoken or written word? I'm not sure that we can; certainly my own understanding of words, in whatever form they are offered, is definitely translated for me by my experiences. I am programmed, I have a mind set, why not you too?

Not only was I drawn away from my progress with the story I promised you by those thoughts about words but also by so many other anecdotes and tales, each with seeming relevance, jostling to be told. I suddenly see quite clearly why SOUL had taken so long to gain my attention. There was always so much to explore, so many interesting side-roads to take, life offered either so many adventures or so many things to occupy my mind that I just didn't leave the tiniest chink where my Soul could creep in. Chink makes me think of armour, armour makes me think of protection and protection makes me think of fear. Soul offers the opposite of fear. Fear is the energy of human existence without Soul knowledge. Soul offers the energy of Unconditional Love, the energy to dispel fear.

I didn't know about that back then where the pattern of my life's experiences were overwhelmingly negative and destructive, inducing in me a state of fear so complete that I didn't even recognise it. I wonder if I have the ability to explain that to you. On the face of it, to state that your very beingness is totally fearful yet not to recognise that condition, to live and function apparently normally while you are consumed by fear, seems at the very least contradictory, at most unbelievable. If you told me the same thing, I'm sure I wouldn't understand.

Here is that word in front of me again, understand: but I am still at the beginning of my tale, so how could you possibly understand me yet? What right have I to expect such a thing from you at this stage?

I'm not sure when it all began, or even if there was a beginning, a start to the process that was to lead me to the space in time when I would hear. No, more than hear. I had always heard and what's more had subconsciously acted upon that hearing. The question was, when I would listen? That's it, the key that opened the door to my Soul was to listen; but listening was not a simple task to do. Something like piano practice or learning to decline Latin verbs when all my mates were off playing on their bikes, when the sun shone all the long day and it took little more than the slightest breeze of opportunity to blow me off course and out to play. After all, didn't the grass of real enjoyment, the freedom of play promise a green-ness even brighter than it appeared?

Stuck; today I'm really stuck here and quite unable to get on with the plot. I've offered the use of myself to the universal energy of Unconditional Love, I sit here with faith and trust that what needs to be written will find its way through the ether and somehow, with almost mystical power, will flow through my openness from my fingertips and onto the screen before me. Nothing is flowing, although my brain hums and tingles with the words and ideas, the thoughts and questions I want to share with you. What I perceived as a simple story has suddenly in the attempt of telling become a complex and tangled web, I seem to be spinning like a frantic fly as the advancing spider wraps his yarns of silk to wind me and bind me into the neat bundle of meat that he can devour. I hear nothing.

Time for some clarity: a recap. What about a trip through the dic.? HEAR *perceive (sound etc.) with the ear*. Fair enough; I had always accepted that my faculties were alert and my brain functioning normally to allow the receiving of sound, but LISTEN *give attention with ear, make effort to hear something*. Well that's it, in a nutshell. I was not giving attention or making effort. Why? Quite simple to answer that, I had absolutely no idea back there that there was anything to be giving attention to or to be making the effort to hear. With hindsight I see that now, but at the time I was blind to it.

So there I was, believing myself to be a normally functioning human being when, as you can already see, I was both deaf and blind. Now I'm wondering, confronted by these revelations, how many more of my senses I had dulled. I will confess to having lost my taste, not in the literal sense, more metaphorical; I had lost my taste for life, for being alive. Well in truth I wasn't very alive. My fears had invaded and then gradually grown, in occupation of my mind, to something disproportionately larger than was healthy. I found myself at the end of a sickeningly destructive marriage, to a violent, mentally ill man; a man, I propose, driven to destruction by fear. Facing aspects of myself in the mirror of that reflected image I had teetered round the rim of self destruction more than once.

When my husband exploded with great style one day, a few weeks after he had relieved me of some teeth that I felt I needed, I was left with a home that resembled more the aftermath of a bomb attack. That should read, left without a home; but with homeless children and family pets. In the nomadic state that followed that particular drama, moving from friend to friend with sufficient material remains of our previous life (large house, good sized farm, and so on) now most preciously carried from place to yet another place in a few bags; in that state of despair yet determination to keep my little family safe and as protected and cared for as was humanly possible, time, uninvited by me into my life, was something I now had.

It's only now, in the process of documenting some of what happened that I understand this. Before the loss of home, of dog and stick farming, of rebuilding neglected barns and buildings, restoring our mediaeval house, rearing, breeding, growing, mowing, combining, carting, caring and playing with the children, the hens, the geese, the goats, the pigeons, the house cow, the piggy pets, growing the fruit, the veg, the flowers; before the loss of all that there simply wasn't any time. Nor did I want there to be.

Some of you will already be a few steps ahead of me, some of you will recognise similar patterns of living, some of you will know that suit of armour; some of you will know that I didn't want any time in which I might have heard, in that silent space, the inner voice. The one we are all blessed with, the one that is there for one reason only; the inner voice, the voice of the Soul that offers Unconditional Love. It offers it in abundance, in excess and superfluity, so much of it that we can take and take for our selves then still have spare to give away. It never dries up, unlike everything else we can both think of, rather the opposite, the more you use the more there is to use.

But as I've already told you, I didn't know about this at the time, not consciously anyway, not in the limited confines of the mind that I was living in. What was wrong with that, it was all I knew, and I wasn't really aware of anyone else living any differently; or was I? It is really strange now to look back. I realise that I was, as we all do, living on two levels. You see the Soul never gives up; it lives its loving way without any acknowledgement from us that it exists. It offered me its help in wisdom, strength, courage, perseverance and hope (characteristics of Unconditional Love) and I used these things unknowingly. I now know, from talking to others, that not only did I take this Unconditional Love for my own use but I gave some of it to them. I often made them feel better or helped them through dark patches, even while experiencing my own life as a sort of hell that I was finding it difficult to escape from. Fear in my being created the hell, my mind and my body experienced it while my Soul just carried on unconditionally loving. Truly amazing.

I can't tell you how lucky, no, how blessed I feel as I write this. While telling you the barest bones of my life's woes, my ever existing memory is filling in the gaps with the gory and hair raising details and it's in these lurid details that I see how my Soul saved me from fates as final as death and I had no idea at all that this was happening, then.

Later, without my home, my animals, my daily round of tasks, anchorless and rudderless, my only drive then to keep my children together in every sense of the word, then there must have appeared a chink in that armour, a gap in my time. If I'd never pondered on the purpose of existence before, though I had, but if I had never, then that was the time to do so, to try and make some sense of my own continuing survival, my existence, my being, and beyond that life in general. We get these chances don't we? The times when the normal routines of our lives stop: death, divorce, illness, accident, any or all of life's dramas and traumas. Some of us don't need a lot of this before we stop short, take notice, take stock, re-evaluate our codes for life, start the search for some higher meaning. Something, anything, just to try and make sense of the tides of human misery and suffering that could easily swamp us if we weakened for a second.

But me, no I hadn't heeded any warnings, I hadn't stopped short to work out what might be going on. Rather the opposite, I donned the mantle of warrior, armed to the teeth, (that was when I still had a full set) dressed up for battle. My war cry, "Hey look at me, I'm here, a sitting target, (but definitely not a sitting duck.) Do your worst, throw the lot at me, (and they very nearly did,) there's nothing you can do that I can't take fair and square, I'm invincible." When I discovered that I wasn't, well, then I had to start all over again, at absolutely everything.

I knew that I had intuition and I used it. I've always firmly believed in the existence of our sixth sense; I'd seen it too often in myself and recognised it so many times in others that denial seemed stupid to me. Why deny anything useful, indeed helpful, just because it's not commonly acknowledged? I could easily reason the loss of our sixth sense, it being our 'natural' sense. Spending most of my days working with nature and knowing myself from the very beginning to be closely in tune with all aspects of the natural world, it appeared glaringly obvious that in civilised (yes, I question that) societies we live about as in touch and in tune with nature as a stone statue on the moon could. So whatever the opposition I stuck, and still stick, to the belief that our sixth sense is alive, (though not so well in a lot of us) and only needs use to see it flourishing.

I like this definition, INTUITION *immediate apprehension by a sense; immediate insight; immediate apprehension by the mind without reasoning,* and apprehension means? You've guessed, understanding; my particular goal you'll recall. Could we be touching here on the essence of my task to unravel the mysteries of the Soul? It has been my experience, both on my own inner and outer life's journeys, that the real understandings of myself, others and life, have not come from words; often words have got in the way. No, definitely not from words but from a true knowing from within, from I believe, the home of the sixth sense, the intuition. That home is within the Soul.

Well that's one of my propositions to you and I'd like to propose something else as we're in that mode; that is, that we could read the word intuition as inner-teaching. Now I know that my brain has the capacity for learning, but teaching, oh no! I cannot accept that that mass of neurons, transmitters, chemicals etc. are teaching me any thing at all. I have come to experience my brain as reactive rather than creative. So if not in my brain, where is this inner part of my being that is offering teachings to me? Simple, I know of no other bodily part that is not already fully deployed on their missions to support my physical being and for that reason it makes absolute sense to me that my Soul is the source of my teaching from within. But I am not setting out here to try to prove or convince you of anything that doesn't sit comfortably with you, only to tell you what I have experienced and the personal insights gained from that.

I firmly believe that truth is as diverse as man himself, that the part of it that we have as an individual is no more than a part; in terms of the millions of us inhabiting this planet, our own truth is but a many-millionth part of the whole truth. I have met people searching for THE TRUTH. I've even been asked if I know what THE TRUTH is. Naturally I said, "Don't be so daft, what reason could there be for The Truth making itself known to me?" but I also said that I did have my own beliefs, which I shared. I did this in the hope that they would share their beliefs with me. If we agree with parts of each other's truth and add these to our own we find a larger helping of The Truth. I love the idea that it is down to each and every one of us to seek out our own truth and to stand by that, acknowledging that the things we believe in are part of the great Truth. There is power in that, man taking responsibility for his self, believing in his individual ability to create something as vitally important as his own truths

In search of my Soul

about anything and everything. TRUTH *a fact or belief that is accepted as true.* BELIEF *an acceptance that something exists or is true, especially one without proof.* (THE TRUTH *that which is true as opposed to false*).

Back then, on my journey, I had no power, no ability to create things as awe inspiring as truths. Oh, I could create artistically, a little musically and a little, a little with words. I could create an enormous amount physically, alter landscapes, re-shape buildings and with some help, deliver new life, but create my truth, no. But with that new gap (time) in my life, it slowly percolated into my demoralised, saddened being that not only might there be something else but that, in order for me to make any sense of my life, there quite simply had to be something else. So the search for that something and my little portion of The Truth began, in earnest.

As I recall how that search began I am experiencing all manner of feelings. For a start I know a slight feeling of panic, I'm looking at the letter keys in front of me and am paralysed by blankness. I really have no idea where to start; no movement from head or fingertips is forthcoming. Have I to abandon my pledge today? The silent one I made to my dear departed friend, the day after his funeral. A silent pledge made in the light of his planned exploits for his future which left this realm as suddenly and unexpectedly as he himself did. Am I to walk away, so soon? I sit quietly, to make contact with my Soul, trusting my belief that the only way I shall understand what is happening and why I am unable to tap the keys today is by listening to the voice of my Soul. So I sit. It is not important that the screen lies blank, even dead, before me. I visualise my Soul, I empty my mind, I speak inwardly, one to the other, acknowledging in doing this the importance of balance and harmony between these two parts of my being: the mortal and the immortal, the material and the non-material; knowing and trusting that this is the only way that I shall find my answer.

That is it, as I experience myself in the act of trusting, my brain registers the word trust, TRUST *firm belief in reliability, honesty, veracity* and so on; the light of understanding floods in. Temporarily today I lost my belief in both something (the value of this book) and in someone (myself) and it was only when I stopped quietly, when I made that chink of space in what we call our time, that I was stilled and quietened enough to listen. I heard the wise voice of my Soul. It said "trust" and then I understood. By feeling my way through the difficulties I was finding getting into my story, by heeding the word of my Soul, my brain started to think about trust. What exactly did that mean and more importantly what did it mean to me? The reacting part of me naturally puts the necessary body systems into action to thumb the alphabet for clarity. That's when the penny drops, that's when I realize that all I am experiencing here and now is the reflection of that time in the past when I began my search. Then I had no firm belief in the reliability of any thing or any one, no belief in justice, no belief in veracity and definitely no confident expectations of anything or anyone, more important, no belief in myself.

My experiences to that date not only within a difficult marriage, but from traumatic childhood times and missed career hopes, to the catastrophic end of our family life, followed by the eye-opening times spent with police and the complexities of our justice systems, those experiences certainly shattered all my naive beliefs of the fairy-tale triumph of good. I'd lost my trust, and in the light of those memories, I recall feeling bloody awful. Well, I said that vehemently, I have no doubt it was true then. Thank goodness there is more to the mind, and that bit more in my mind, that Soul of mine, of whose existence I had no knowledge, well that, and the power it exerts spurred me to look for something else. Something that was to slowly (most of the time far too slowly for my impatient nature) but surely lead me back to the place of belief and trust that I had enjoyed before I allowed life's little thunderbolts to knock the stuffing out of me.

An opportunity quickly presented itself. An advert appeared from someone wanting to start a development circle. I had had a previous interest in astrology, a dabble at divvying, some truly desperate visits to mediums, tarot readers etc., none of which were accurate or helpful in my direst hours of need. One particular person gave me the most dangerous (and inaccurate) advice imaginable, which, though so unhelpful at the time, taught me one of my most valuable lessons. I decided I would never make any attempt at fortune telling, at prophecies, whatever you want to call it. Even more important I would strive at all times to avoid telling anyone what to do however much I was tempted to do that.

'Development' though; my curiosity was aroused and I became part of a new group which found its way to my temporary home and the next one as well, and left me years later and many groups further on with friends in my phone book. I didn't know where I was going or what I hoped to learn. I didn't really know what a development circle was; something to do with being psychic wasn't it? What was psychic? PSYCHIC (force) *non-physical force, assumed to explain spiritualistic phenomena.* Hmmph! I don't much like the sound of that. A therapist I saw once was very insistent that to 'assume' makes an 'ass of u and me'. I was never quite sure how I felt about that, but I am sure that assumption denotes some popular opinion rather than tried and tested fact. Thus I am no closer to fully understanding that word psychic and I need to acquaint myself with spiritualistic as that word really conveys nothing clearly to me either. SPIRITUALISTIC .... having offered the word as part of the definition of psychic my dictionary describes this as a derivative of spiritualism.

In search of my Soul

No wonder at the outset I had uncertainties. At that stage I was ignorant of the multitude of meanings and understandings of those two important words, psychic and spiritual. Later I was to find that there were times when they appeared synonymous, and conversely times when they seemed as far removed from each other as possible. I think that was, and is, reflective of our difficulties as we search for the unknown; along the way of that searching we are called upon to abandon rationality and reason, we are called to accept unusual happenings and experiences that definitely defy logic, sometimes magical, sometimes mysterious, sometimes even miraculous. Happenings that in recounting usually begin, "I know this sounds unbelievable, but," and that drew from my children the partly teasing, the partly seriously worried line, "oh no, mother's off to loony-go-round again." I was.

I continued my quest to find answers to my unasked questions, to find the key to the mystery of life, to discover above everything else the supremely wise person I knew existed. This person I firmly believed would, when I caught up with him, furnish me not only with answers but with knowledge and wisdom which I would be able to use for myself. Perhaps this was my ultimate goal way back then. I know, looking back there now, that I had no idea at all that all the things that seemed so important for me to find, in order really just to survive, were within me.

The search for this other person was the drive needed to get me travelling a new road; my conviction in the existence of this person was invincible (although along the long, long road it got rather shaky.) So, I searched, and searched and then searched some more. From circle to another circle; sometimes meditation, Buddhist, Transcendental, sitting rooms, guided, not guided, with music, with water, with dolphins, with gongs, with Tibetan bowls, hugging a tree, candles, incense, crystals; you think of it and I tried it, and always the tea and bickies to follow. At one group I went to every week for more than two years the host gave us delicious choc and nut hob-nobs, the like of which were never afforded at home, though I'm not saying that's why I went regularly for so long. Yet more circles, sometimes development, medium-ship training, spiritualism (communication with the spirits of the deceased) spiritual healing, divination. DIVINATION *insight into, discovery of the unknown or the future by supernatural means* and workshop to another workshop, lectures, classes, the College of This and the School of That. If money had not been a problem I would have spent a gold mine, as it was I spent a mint. Doubtless I learned something I needed to know wherever I went, though it felt at the time that whenever I thought myself to be getting just that little bit closer to the target, well, it moved, in most cases it disappeared entirely. Those were bad times. Yes, I know I was impatient and on the vast stage of time a group that flourished for more than two years was a mere millisecond in time's reality, but the waiting in between at my journey's bus stops for the next vehicle ("will there be another one?") seemed endless.

I have always had a rather vivid creative imagination. My mother always chided (that's the polite version) me for "reaching for the stars instead of getting on with what's under your nose" (which was always some job or chore that she felt was far more worthy of my attention.) Well, my imagination managed to create scenarios of potential possibilities from even the tiniest new thing that came my way; consequently I was quadruply more disheartened to find myself at those bus stops than I would have been had I just taken everything at face value and not been busily building castles in the air. Beautiful constructions they were.

Naturally everywhere I went I met new faces, obvious to me now, just like me they were searching for their answers, their portion of The Truth, but there and then it was not so obvious. Oh, I could feel the suffering, tune into that OK through prison walls, that's something I'd always known, the silent inner sufferings of others, I could always feel what was going on inside. I didn't court that, who would, for the music that tugged my heart strings was never their joy always their pain; I'm not saying that the world's woes gravitated to me, but I was certainly aware of plenty of it about.

Then I was functioning at the ego level, (EGO *individuality, part of the mind that reacts to reality, and has sense of self-esteem*) experiencing most of these new things, ideas and people, very much in an intellectual state of mind; a state, which I have since learnt, holds our negative experiences and seems to have an over-riding mindset of fear. Fear operating on every level of thought and therefore governing every level of action from the simple 'how do I look? are these clothes the right sort of thing to wear? will I know anyone there? will anyone want to talk to me? will I be OK if I have to speak? will I go puce with embarrassment? do I really want to go? will I trip on the steps? will I manage to make myself look stupid in front of the people I'd like to impress?' to the complex. The complex? I find I can't list those, for my belief is that when you really listen you see beneath the surface and discover that those seemingly trite worries are really the outer clothing of deeply held, unresolved, complex issues. Then though, I wasn't into really listening. I would have protested vehemently if you had suggested that, because I cared so much, for people (especially those in any sort of trouble) for the world of nature in whatever form, for anything and everything you can think of, and my caring could be seen and heard. But it was almost as if I was two people. Did the insights, the understanding of things not overt, go unheeded as they pricked too gently at my mind; or did they bombard and batter the fear of my unbalanced mind-set too loudly thus causing my inner wisdom to go unheard?

Yet I learnt wherever I went; sometimes about myself, sometimes about others. I learnt a lot about how others saw their possibilities in life. I read a lot with great interest, trying to understand other people's truths; much of the time I didn't understand any of it, yet those I met seemed so positive. They were glowing with their discoveries, a new teacher, new guru, new spiritual leader, new therapies everywhere; have you been to this? have you done that? have you tried the other? and each time such acclaim for the newest answer, the latest way. Had I read the latest book? (no can't afford it) Have you got the latest tape? (no can't afford it) Have you been to so and so's workshop? (no can't afford it) Are you eating this? Rubbing yourself with that? and so on and ever more on (no I can't afford it.)

A message was coming through loud and clear but I wasn't ready yet to listen to it, instead my negative mind, my fear, worked away to leave me feeling that I really didn't fit there with those people. It was as if, in not being able to experience the material peripheral trappings on that searching pathway, I experienced myself as somehow lacking; I was an outsider not quite comfortable with those around me, a sort of infiltrator who might be rumbled at any moment. Have you any idea how much I wanted to belong, to be part of these apparently cosy, convivial groups? I didn't belong and own up here to having never felt truly comfortable or at ease. I had no idea why. Many years later I have plenty of ideas and I know now that the important lesson I was learning was that I could stand alone, if you like, be brave enough to say "No. However good things look, however right for another, those things are not right for me." It's easy now, now I know what I don't want and know the things that are not right for me, but back then it was extremely painful.

Still my searching continued, and I set off optimistically on any and every new road that opened up before me, still with that fertile imagination running riot, always light years ahead of myself, constructing visions, dreams and fantasies. I don't knock that, it was what kept me going in one sense. Each time a new road evaporated before me the creative part of my mind spurred me ever onward, what I never knew then was that it was the creative part of my Soul that was doing the pushing. I am in no doubt that without that I would have given up. That's the beauty of the Soul it does its work uninvited; it carries on unencouraged. What a friend to have. I didn't recognise that, then.......

Do you know, as I think back I cannot recall anyone at all ever mentioning the word Soul, never suggesting its existence, never any acknowledgement; yet wasn't I on a 'spiritual' journey, hoping for enlightenment, searching for something 'out of this world', outside myself? Yes I was, still hot on the trail of the believed in wise person who would give me all the answers, and boy did I have a mountain of questions. For it seemed that every time I thought that I had really learnt something, my inquiring curiosity popped up myriad mysteries that no book, no teacher, no believed-to-be-at-the time wise person could satisfy.

Then there were all the really weird things, ascensions, fifth-dimensions, inter galactic beings, mediums speaking the tongues of alien races, all alien to me. Don't misunderstand me here. I'm not knocking that. Each to his own is my motto as long as it harms no-one else. I have lived too long and seen too many things not to have learnt that one man's meat is indeed another's poison (as long as I did not have to eat perceived poison.) I honour the right of every individual to live by his own belief; I am, after all, the person who not so long ago proposed that truth is personal. I really believe that, as I did then, which of course made it easier for me to live and let live (although it didn't go any where to fostering my own sense of belonging.)

I met some really nice people. My old head-mistress would have stiffened at the use of that word of 'no literary value.' NICE [colloq.] *kind, friendly, agreeable, considerate, etc.,* that's exactly the sentiments I wish to express. Nice people who in their caring for their fellows were looking for ways to find peace, to heal themselves and others, to take more care of the planet and all that inhabit it. Yes, I met many very nice people, so why oh why was I never, quite, perfectly comfortable?

And then a very long wait at one of those bus stops. So long in fact that I felt that I'd become invisible along with my next transport, and I wandered off. Well many years had passed since I'd set out, life had taken more twists and turns, and I found myself a mother again at such a ripe old age that the official title on my records at the maternity hospital recorded 'ancient multi-pod'. The young, very young nurses called me "miracle mum", which I rather preferred, though even that small claim to fame has now been eclipsed.

During these years I had returned to some of the interests of my pre farmer's wife days, working as an interior designer, some garden designing, joined a choir, tried to play the piano again, kept up the drawing and painting and creative embroidery. My new home was, and still is, an old farmhouse in need of much restoration work. You might have thought that was enough to keep me busy, and in a way it was; there were many times I was too busy. Yet, yes, you know, still there, nagging away was that big question. What's it all about?

You see, along my road I had rubbed shoulders with so many people who had found value in what they had learned, had pursued their dream, had developed their abilities and then moved on to help others. That's what I wanted to do, help others, and I could. I could do any of the things that they were doing, but I wasn't; somehow I could not pursue any of the things I saw others being so successful, fulfilled and happy to be doing. I wished I could, yet for reasons,

In search of my Soul

I couldn't, and I was so envious (in the best way I knew how.) All that and more was still there. I started to feel trapped by so many years of motherhood and the daily domestic grind. The interests and all those extras didn't fill the hole I felt inside. However over-full or over-busy my life, that hole yawned. I could not find satisfaction with myself.

Still looking for the truth that would satisfy me off I went again, with the same questions, in pursuit of some answers, but this time in a completely different direction.

Did I mention that I had always been fascinated by people, curious to know what made the individual tick, the hows, whys and wherefores of their lives? More especially I suppose I wanted to understand the inner man or woman because I had always felt so aware of that part of people, the part that really people didn't seem to want to talk about. I was puzzled by this knowing, mostly because it seemed to be quite without purpose. Yes, if it was at all appropriate I could share the awareness; sometimes it was, sometimes I did, but all I learnt from that was that a trouble shared is not a trouble halved, but a trouble declared, acknowledged. Giving 'pain' the light of day was not much use to either party and I grew to feel particularly frustrated by my complete inability to offer anything helpful or useful in these situations.

Actually I wanted this phenomenon to go away and leave me alone, for I had enough buried pain of my own, and picking up other people's as well was really leading to overload. I hadn't learnt then that it was only the mire of my misfortunes, hidden so deeply in unfelt buried pain that enabled me to find the pain in others. The only way to consciously experience my pain was to feel it in others, they were the mirror for me; but I wasn't looking. Small wonder then that I wished the insights would stop; 'my gift' was unusable, it was a relentless taunt. Often I would find myself with an extra burden and it wasn't mine; naturally I didn't look for this, it was completely involuntary. Then when I tried to make use of the gift I found that I had no idea what to do with it, the more cross I got about this the more people found their way to my door; more than that, into my home and into my life.

As the problems and pain grew my frustration grew too, along with my sense of inadequacy. It may seem unbelievable to you that I didn't see what was going on. I didn't see the lesson that was being offered, no, shoved at me. I was still blind, deaf, dumb, and stupid; though I told myself so many times what a slow learner I was, that didn't speed up the process. I just didn't see that all these people were in fact coming to help me, not as I thought, looking for me to make everything better for them; coming before me, not to taunt me with my own uselessness but to mirror for me my own inner suffering, which I was still utterly unaware that I had. Naturally, being blind to my own situation, I had no idea that it was me who needed the help, me who needed restoring to healthy, harmonious balance; even though the outer me, my shell, my body was constantly racked with discomfort and pain I remained in ignorance of my inner pain.

Looking back I cannot believe how blind I was, me the observant one, the noticer of details, the discoverer of nature's minute hidden gems, the person who saw all and nothing, at the same time. Least of all did I have any understanding of the truth that I was going to learn...eventually.... Part of my own truth, and I want to suggest to you, part of The Truth and that is that all healing comes from within. Individuals are not healers, they are catalysts (keys, enablers, channels, ways, whatever.) It is the Soul that heals with Unconditional Love. I say emphatically from my experiences, the Soul is the way of healing power.

I'm back, but of course you didn't know that I was gone, such is the power of the written page covering (or is it failing to reveal) the contents of spaces in time. Time is a strange phenomenon. This is a subject I'm sure that we could delve deeply into, but not now. Today the date is 10.01.2000 and as I said I've been away. To be precise, just away from this machine.

I wish I had been away; holidays have never featured large in my life. My childhood was a little bare in that department, without a father around money and opportunities were rare. To put things into perspective, only the 'better off' families regularly went away and I certainly never heard much news of holidays abroad.

Some things remain brightly in my memory. My first seaside holiday with a school friend's family in a caravan; driving there in an old open top car I think we sort of spilled over as we bobbed along, three children, parents, luggage, all rattling with excitement and anticipation (perhaps I was the only one spilling over as they'd done it all before.) The week was, as all good memories tell, sun-filled, with sea, sand, friend and family.

I did have a favourite Aunt, I think I was favoured in return; she had two boys and I learnt much later in my life that she would dearly have loved a little girl like me. With this Aunt and Uncle there were times spent at their home on the edge of the New Forest. They had a car and were more than happy to indulge my ravenous appetite for all things old, ancient monuments, burial mounds, castles, museums and any scenic attraction within a day's radius; that wasn't so far in those days of the steam car. I never remember breaking down, mostly due I suspect to the care and attention given to that family car in those early days of motoring. I am wondering now as I recall happy days whether they enjoyed all the adventurous outings as much as I did, or whether their enjoyment mostly came from sharing my obvious delight in the things they were able to show me. That's very often the quality of enjoyment isn't it? I confess to you now that I took full advantage of the spoiling I received, though I never quite got used to the gentle patting with a warm towel at bathtime, somehow I was never quite sure that I was truly dry as the technique was at variance with the one employed by my mother at home.

But, back to today, now a month since I was here last. I knew that it would be difficult to keep to my promise of an hour's writing a day come what may. At the beginning of my son's Christmas holiday I started as I meant to go on, but with more of the family taking extended time off I realised that my intentions were unrealistic; best to shut down completely and make a new start later. This is the new start; it has to be that as I have no knowledge of how far I got last year.

I don't think I explained exactly what prompted me to make the original start. It began with the death of a dear friend, a friendship that had spanned the individual journeys of our two lives over four and a half decades, often with large gaps in between; but spanned and survived it did, until suddenly, totally unexpectedly death stepped in. I experienced all the usual symptoms, regrets being one of the things that featured prominently. At our age retirement is on the horizon and plans for the new found freedom this promises were talked about just before he died. To be truthful I was a tad cynical as in my position, with an eleven year old lively son, retirement is absolutely the last thing on my mind, so I had done a little of my usual leg pulling. This was doubtless tinged with envy; wouldn't I like the chance of a cottage-by-the-sea, free time and money to pursue the hobbies and pleasures which we all plan to, one day? Now I regret the envy, I'm here with the chance, he is not.

It was thoughts in this vein, whirling around in the 'daze' of disbelief after his death, that suddenly gathered them-selves into a decision. I resolved there and then to do something that I had started to do a few times before (I still have the sheets and exercise books full to prove that.) I would stop prevaricating. I would do it. I would write a book and I would stick at it until I had succeeded; this time there would be no giving up, no excuse for side-tracking, no pastures new would beckon (well they might but no way would they be heeded.) Whatever insecurities, doubts, put downs or anything else that I, or indeed anyone, could conjure up to break my resolve, this time I would succeed. The reason for this is that this time I would be doing it for someone else. I declared to myself that, in honour of my friend's life and as a mark of respect for his supportive, undemanding friendship, I would persevere and not give up until I had reached my goal.

I know this is something that I have done many times before, given up before reaching my goal. No matter how near the goal may have been, no matter how certain reaching it seemed, if it was really something for myself, for my well-being, then you can be sure that I never made it. The reasons for that are, like all reasons for anything that holds me (and you) back from personal fulfilment, held in the past and maintained by the repeating patterns of negative events. These feed the fearful mind, each time reconfirming its long held beliefs. I see that I said 'are', I should have said 'were' (old habits really do die hard, I have to keep ever watchful and keenly listening to maintain the changes I've set in motion.) I see also that I told you that I am writing my book for someone else; that is not correct either.

Of course I am writing it for my satisfaction, for my own inner wellbeing, for my Soul, so why did I put it to you that this could only be achieved for someone else? The old conditioning of my mind speaking then, so may I rephrase the statement? My resolve to write is my own; there is absolutely no doubt in me that I had reached a state of being in which I had enough contact with my own source of power (my Soul) to enable an overriding of my mind's negative fear system which had previously managed to prevent me accomplishing such 'fanciful ideas'. Some of the crap of the past (I call these Soul Shadows) has, to my untold delight, GONE. And my friends part in this? Answer: at the right time in my life, that is, at the very time that I was learning about Unconditional Love and therefor was in a position to recognise it, he offered it. I took it. I cannot return it now in any other way than to offer it through this book that I have dedicated to him. Unconditional Love (this will be a recurring theme.) Unconditional Love the powerful, final piece in that particular jigsaw.

Thinking back, especially on the theme of unfinished schemes, I can vividly recall the excitement in my being each time in my life that a new idea struck. As we're discussing the birthing of this book I am remembering the others I tried to hatch. It was always such a 'growing' experience, the sensation of being filled with the inspiration of ideas, words and illustrations; the print, the cover, the glowing introductory passage by a famous person, the ensuing fame. Was it all about fame FAME *the state of being famous*. FAMOUS *known about by many people*, or just part of my quest to be heard? To be known and in that to be respected? Is that why I never succeeded? Yes. Now I know that success and absolutely everything else that has true worth comes from within; in the light of my own experiences, the 'within' that comes from is my Soul.

I could never really understand why my writings didn't get anywhere, I felt instinctively that I could be on to a 'winner'; I thought I had the ability, and if ideas, dreams and schemes were anything to go by, well, I had those in excess. I began in earnest one year documenting month by month the flowers that paraded the banks and ditches of our mile long farm track. I listed, drew and

In search of my Soul

painted, adding birds, butterflies, anything, with little anecdotes of the changing seasons, the sights, sounds and smells in this wonderland of nature. I recounted the tale of the white pheasant who survived two winters living in a heap of brushwood, a solitary, isolated existence owing to his difference and in this his unacceptability; an outcast of his species, but what joy he lent us and what loss when his pure snowy silhouette no longer topped the dull, lifeless branches. I told of the farmer, who swapped and tidied those verges and ditches on the mile long drive, a solitary figure also in his toil, and isolated in his existence by his blindness, but (and this was the point of my telling) he never cut himself, he never harmed any creature or flower and I swear (from our storytelling and note swapping) that he saw as much as me.

But, there was no book and a few years after that I noticed a spate of similarly based works become quite popular in the bookshops.

I made quite a good attempt at a baby book, a dictionary of childbirth, with plenty of reality, understandable information and a good dose of humour. Having literally 'hatched' five times, and survived the gamut of bringing new life, even death, into this world, I felt confident that I had a lot to offer. I spent far more time in hospital last time round, waiting for the day when my lastborn child would emerge from his incubator and finally say goodbye to the congenital pneumonia that he had arrived with; during this time my inspiration was awesome. I would wake in the night and find myself pouring with the words that were rushing so fast into my head. I thought "if I don't let all this out I shall burst". The elation was euphoric. I knew that I was almost experiencing mania yet it felt so indescribably good, I felt so strong. It was an insight that I am grateful to have had, for it gave me an understanding of how it might be for those who suffer from manic depression. Knowing the powerful surge of well-being I felt in the high swing I can quite understand how this may convince some-one that they were God (by that I mean, all powerful.)

I believe my family were concerned by the obvious elation and over the top well-being, worrying that it was a form of post-natal depression, but I had other ideas. I knew that I had no depressive illness, after all depression and me were almost bedfellows. I suspected (for reasons totally unknown to me at that time) that I was being shown creativity in the raw. I truly felt that at that time I knew exactly how a genius felt when a great symphony burst from him or a work of art appeared at his fingertips. It was wonderful and was perhaps the first time that I could feel that there was more to my being than the mind that I thought was me.

That was eleven years ago, it was still to take a lot more signs before this stubborn one woke up. That creation did not manifest either, despite much help from matron and staff who took my intentions seriously and supplied me with a lot of clinical details and articles to study. I intended to seek Royal

Soul Listening

patronage for the book, but as the creative mania declined so did my resolve. You know what I'm going to tell you now. Some time after this there was a boom in baby literature not dissimilar to my proposed offering.

And so I went on following the old pattern of giving up. My most recently 'given up' literary attempt was a more personal work tracing my life, (I had convinced myself that it might be of some interest to others) but the rot set in and when I looked at what I'd written I could see no value in it, despite the enticing title The Diary of Another Nobody. I was never short of titles, and could think up more of those than of interesting subject matter. I kept going a while, in fits and starts, scribbling page after page after page. I thought of beginnings and endings, dedications and introductions, but what was the middle about? I saw analogy upon analogy, vibrant pictures in my mind, clever words, very telling, deep philosophical stuff but it came out kitchen sink variety. I tried structure, form, purpose and plot.

The only picture I saw was a plate of spaghetti. My life is like a plate of spaghetti. How would that be for openers, and could I develop that theme into a structure that would support the events of my life? It seemed all far too boring, in fact as I looked I realised that what the tangled pasta needed was some sauce, that always makes a popular read, but it's not me. That tangled lump of pasta strands, could indeed be a life, all those threads, woven in and out, out and in, sometime touching, sometime not, leave it to cool a little and all would be congealed in one glutinous mass, or is it mess? Yes, that could easily be the representation of my life. How do I sort that to write about it? No sooner had I started exploring one strand than I was entangled with another. Do I follow the same strand on its journey or do I trek off with the new one, or do I extricate each and every single strand and lay them side by side in their soldierly rows? That would certainly be easier, but the story would be all endings and beginnings, incoherent and disjointed.

I think it was about this time that I gave up the idea of writing my book. It was becoming more and more difficult; I couldn't conceive a format let alone a plot. It seemed so pointless and at the end of the day a useless exercise; hadn't I previously given up when the odds were far more favourable? Time for something new I decided. Time for something practical.

Money seemed to be a recurring theme on the domestic front, lack of it and my own inability to contribute much to the family coffers. I have tried, in the past two or three years I tried very hard to find a job. Nobody wants a woman of my years without paper qualifications. You may have experienced this. The years of useful and meaningful study in the University of Life count for nought. How to earn an honest penny or two? Most jobs require computer skills, which

In search of my Soul

I don't have. I must set up my own business, the avenue for that has to be the Internet, but whatever can I do?

All of which sends me back to rue my total lack of computer skills and seek some solution. Being short of money means I must be my own tutor, so, armed with the Idiots Guide to the Mac, I closet myself in the 'office' and begin, and end, in tears of frustration, with the certain knowledge that I am indeed that 'idiot' referred to. I persevere, slowly, painstakingly, but surely. I teach myself to switch ON and OFF. It is somewhere in the middle of this struggle to equip myself for a job (in this technological age) with income, that my friend dies, and somewhere in the aftermath of that event that I found myself sitting in front of this screen armed with a pledge and a resolve, and very little else.

That's where I began, painstakingly tapping out the letters, trying to keep the type in order, and very slowly learning how to manoeuvre my way around the keyboard gizmos. I don't know what that means but it feels right, gizmos they are when I try any sort of text correcting or manipulation and everything goes into chaos in front of me. Thus, I'm not manipulating, inserting, cutting or correcting, just concentrating on the tapping. When it was discovered that 'mother is writing', and, incredulously, 'on the computer', (for they had all witnessed the tear-stained aftermath of my DIY tuition sessions) some questions were asked. "Whatever have you got to write about? Is it for your own amusement? Surely you're not thinking it will be published?" What could I say? The truth. Which was "I'm just tapping, having a go really, rather than just talking of things which might or might not be done some day, somewhere in the future." They didn't believe that I was just tapping, but I was. It took so much concentration on my part even to work the machine and plenty more to find the keys (although I play the piano occasionally I've never learnt to type) that every scrap of brain power was in use.

It was only when I got some help to show me how to find what I'd formed and then how to put it away and then how to get it out the next day to add to it, that I read what I'd written at the beginning. This was in capitals actually, as somehow I'd engaged that lock and hadn't realised until much later when I raised my eyes from the keyboard to appraise my handiwork. TO GO WITH SOUL. I didn't really know what that meant, it had come to me and I'd tapped it; but working with Soul and pursuing my theories about the existence and the purpose of my own for the last two years gave me a pretty good idea of what was going on. So I told the family, "It's a Soul book." They understood, having heard very little else from me in that time and having taken part in some of the experiments that were to prove my theories to me. (Yes, to me, not to them; remember this is the family who find their mother, in their politest terms, weird.)

They understood the cause but not the effect, as I really couldn't tell them any more that made acceptable sense to them. I truly was just tapping, with no thought of plot, no plan of format and you could say, no idea what I was really doing. Each day I placed myself in front of the screen (as I still do) and the tapping is not much quicker or easier than it was in the beginning, and still I rarely look at the screen. I sit, not thinking and definitely never knowing where the tapping will lead me. When I first saw the word SOUL I knew that whatever was to be achieved, or whatever had to be done, it would be achieved through trust and would be done by the wisdom of my Soul. The minute I acknowledged that in this venture I am little more than a willing servant, I understood the words 'to go with soul.'

That is exactly what I have been learning to do with my theories and inner journeys of discovery. That is exactly what I am doing in writing this. I have complete trust in the infinite wisdom of my Soul; my mind does not need the over-riding involvement in this writing that I previously believed would be necessary; I can use my brain for the spelling and machine work but the content; that comes from the Soul. Can I prove that to you? Do I want to? Probably 'no' to both. I have already told you my belief that truth is individual, truth is our own, and anything I propose here I acknowledged as my own truth only.

It is offered with Unconditional Love, Soul love, in case any of the miraculous things that I have witnessed and experienced while working with Souls can be your truth also. I do hope so, isn't that after all the sole[?] purpose of this book?

My personal proof that the tapped words come from the Soul: I have written acres of longhand, letters, studying and those books notes I've been telling you about, so longhand comes easily to me. I can write almost as quickly as I think. Writing like that is a completely automatic process, thus leaving plenty of spare brain power. Yet to write the 'Soul book' I sit at a machine I can only just switch on, one that takes all my concentration and all my brain power to operate. If I needed proof, this is it. It is as if the only method for my brain to let go the reins of the writing process would be if it were totally occupied by something else. My mind just needs that quiet space, that gap in its normal frantic buzzing to enable it to hear the words of my Soul.

Not that this harmony could have existed if I had not reached a place of trust, which I guess must have been achieved by my previous acknowledgements, not just of the existence of Soul, but of its role in my being as the other half of me, the positive, powerful, creative half with its magnificent energy of Unconditional Love. The Soul is the source of the energy of Unconditional Love, the brain is the source of the energy of fear and the mind is home to both. A bold statement of personal belief; I hope the tales I share illustrate for you how I arrived at this.

In search of my Soul

I see those words now and wonder however has my story found its way from where I thought I was to where I am now; I don't recall where or when I wandered away from the train of events I was recounting.

Now something extraordinary is happening in front of me, things are all over the place. I wonder did my negative mind try to take over the process of this writing, for certainly the mechanics of the tapping, which has till now been easy and most absorbing, suddenly became very difficult, letters and words splitting off, moving apart, dropping out of sight or onto another row.

I didn't tap any more yesterday, despite my vow to do at least an hour each day. Suddenly I lost it. It was the sight of the fragmentation of the type in front of me, then my total inability to gather it back into any sort of coherent order, that freaked me out. I knew something was happening. Something was being shown to me. By that I mean that an opportunity was being offered for me to learn something, to gain an insight, to see something (that was, on the face of it, a manifestation of my shortcomings in the computer skills department) in a completely different light. So I shut down the machine for the day and resumed my normal home mode, knowing from previous experiences that even the smallest (and hitherto un-noticed) hiccups in my life (and by association, in everyone else's) are an opportunity to discover more about the workings of my mind. I know that presented as hiccups these workings are negative ones, setbacks. I discovered nothing that day. Sometimes it can be quite a while for the significance of events to dawn on me, but dawn they do, without fail. If I listen for the wise voice of my Soul, I will hear it.

It took a little practice at first, sometimes it didn't work, due to the state of my mind. I've always been a very slow learner, a cynic perhaps. I needed a lot of convincing. Sometimes I lost heart, I didn't practice. Sometimes I lost my trust in my developing beliefs, never totally, although I have come pretty close to it. Thankfully now I know that I have a Soul, now I know what it is for and how to use it, now I have much more trust in my belief. Enlightenment on this occasion was not instant, but that didn't matter. I just left the question hanging in my mind until the 'light dawned' as I knew it would. It's a fabulous feeling, that confident, knowing certainty.

In the life I've known there has not been too much certainty; perhaps that's a silly thing to say as we all know that the one certain thing we can expect in life is uncertainty. Rather, there has been very little knowing. I'm now trying to recall anything that I can honestly say I know for certain. The things that come to mind are all to do with nature and the elements. I've never seen rain going upwards, the sun shine at dark of night, I've not seen a fish swim the fields or summer flowers in the snow. Anything else and I can't find the certainty. Do we know for certain that we will wake in the morning? Do we know for certain that we will return from our journey? Maybe the two most pertinent of our uncertainties, will our love last, will we find happiness? Happiness, health and love, things we all hope for and things that are absolutely uncertain. Is it any wonder that we exist in a state of fear? The precarious nature of survival alone is daunting; it doesn't do to think too deeply about it. Add to that the traumas of our raising and, even without bringing the Soul memories of previous existences and deaths into this equation, we are faced with a built-in baggage of fearful uncertainties. Yet in the face of all this I am telling you about the knowing certainty that is to be found. I am finding it in myself. By association, as we are potentially all the same, it is to be found in all of us.

My knowing arrived next day as I recounted my manual mis-deavors, voicing aloud my belief that something could be learnt from those, reconfirming my belief that the knowledge would present itself in due course. That was when I saw the message. Somehow yesterday I had given the major share of involvement in this writing back to the ego of my mind. Looking back now I remember engaging my mind in certain processes, perhaps the significant one being the questioning; those self doubt, lack of confidence questions, the ones that really illustrate the negative power of the fearful mind. I started to try and think the words, the plot and the purpose. If you like I started to look for my importance, the ego-mind importance and hey presto all concentration on the tapping task was lost; so clear to me now. At another level (these things always come layer upon layer) I could understand and see (as I'd seen the chaotic type in front of me the day before) that in life, as on the screen, if the brain does not have harmony and balance with the Soul then mind disorder and mayhem are the consequence. In the light of this understanding I resolve to watch my step tomorrow.

The really joyous thing in all this is that I know that if I listen to the wisdom of my Soul it always, unfailingly and with complete certainty tells me the answers. I thank my Soul as usual. A cursory passing nod, it doesn't require great ceremony or ritual any more than any of my physical organs do to keep them working efficiently. My Soul asks only sensible practical care and attention, the sort that any person gives to any other part of his body that he has respect for.

I'm asking myself today, where am I? The feelings I have are those of slight bewilderment. I'm a bit lost. I suppose that's exactly how I was feeling waiting at that stop by my roadside, waiting for the next step along my own particular highway of life to signpost itself. I was feeling lost, yet again I had turned my back on something that had seemed so full of promise in my imaginative mind.

In search of my Soul

Fulfilment, even success had seemed a possibility. The reality was that nothing lived up to my expectations. The openings and opportunities I dreamed of were just that, dreams. Had my mother been right after all? Was I just chasing stars that were way beyond my reach? Hadn't I been watching people with no more 'talent' than my own, reach goals that I could only see, never actually touch?

Yes only slightly lost, never so completely lost that I couldn't see a glimmer of opportunity when it showed itself. Very soon I was having an interview for a course of training which would lead me to work, with people, in the 'caring' sector. Psychodynamic Counsellor. Now that was a title of some importance, wasn't it? Why the handle itself is twenty-three letters long. I mean, I couldn't be a plain ordinary counsellor could I? Not when what I really wanted to be was at the very least a clinical psychologist, (or perhaps I could have accepted psychotherapist.) But I'd not made those dizzy heights, despite certain ability. I'd done my psychology 'A' level at evening classes, tried to get to university to do the degree in same, but the practicalities (mostly revolving round time and money) loomed too large for me.

Now those of you who understand how things really work in life will be shaking your heads in a knowing way, telling me that I really didn't want to do this thing as badly as I thought I did. Of course in part you are right, but I didn't know that at the time and was naturally sorely peeked at being kept from my dream, my goal. I said you are partly right; I want to explain how I view that scenario now, as it has repeated itself many times in order to be 'seen'.

My mind, in those days would quite truthfully tell me that this was my path. I had the ability, the drive, the desire, everything but the one vital element. I believed it was where I should and could be. However as I've said already, my mind was ruled by an ego coloured by my negative experiences, it functioned from need, the need being fed by fear. The whole process is a vicious circle, with fear very much in charge. When the needs are not fulfilled, as they were not each time I failed at the latest dream-goal chasing, the thing that I was driving myself to overcome in the first place came full circle to confront me again and again. Face on. So it was that I ventured off to put my talents to perceived good use, to win from outside the acclaim that I so needed, thinking then that outside praise, a position of some importance, a place where I could be seen and heard, would make all well inside. I would be able to feel good about myself at last. Remember though that consciously I was not ware that it didn't feel good to be me, which may explain why I ended up each time with nothing but my NEED staring me in the face.

I completed the round of need time and time again, but still did not see what was being thrown at me. Every time I failed to reach my goal my belief in my own unworthiness was re-confirmed and so every time I set off in search of outside approval I was on a hiding to nothing. What a lot of grief I could have saved myself had I had any inkling of the mysterious processes that were playing themselves out in my being (they are doing that in yours too.) We become human needings, which in turn leads to human-doings, doing to drive away our needing. The answer is to be, just 'be' and so experience the human 'being'. More of that later.

For now I found myself off on the next tack in my search for the success that would lead to self approval. I had not found it in my spiritual adventures. I would turn my back on that and go for the more tried and tested clinical route, maybe that would open up some doors, and show me 'my place'. Foolish girl, I still wasn't completely listening, though in truth it is impossible to listen until the time comes when you realize, acknowledge and then KNOW that there is actually something to listen to.

Remembering back to that interview I can still clearly hear myself telling the nice lady, that I had dealt with any problems that I might have had as a result of my father being 'mentally ill' all my life, and not being around; my confidence no doubt linked to my slight forays into Freud *et al* and 'abnormal psychology'. Place that bold statement against its true background, where my Dad was mysteriously whisked from the face of the earth one day while I was taken to the park, where his non-existence was not explained, not even mentioned and where the subsequent years found me telling any new acquaintance that "I haven't got a father" and sincerely believing in that telling, and you see the incongruity. I was well into my teens and, if not actually verbalising the score, still living with that belief although I had been taken to visit him in his incarceration. (What a bloody damned awful place mental hospitals were; I thought many times that if you weren't deranged when you went into one, you very soon would be.) There had even been times when he came home, causing havoc and mayhem with his so-titled 'lunatic' behaviour; LUNATIC insane, mad INSANE, *not of sound mind, mentally deranged, extremely foolish, irrational* (a lot of words there to try to convey a true understanding of the 'mentally ill' label) like the night when he would have throttled my mother, had her own mother not been miraculously staying with us.

Later when he was moved four counties to another asylum near his parents I could quite honestly keep up my belief in having no Dad.

So, having placed myself into the healthy (Latin, sanus, hence in-sane, unhealthy) category, I was an ideal candidate to set about unravelling the mysteries of all the minds of those troubled people who would be clamouring for the attention of my trained and informed Psychodynamic Counsellor's mind. Look what I would be charging them!

I hope my undisguised sarcasm is not screaming out prejudice. It's definitely not that; it is frustration born out of helplessness which I am now recalling as my mind fills with the images and memories of those occasions when

In search of my Soul

my father was in my life. Each incident is laden with emotions, and that is exactly what came to the fore during my studying and training; frightening emotions. It was horrible, yet no-one could tell me what to do with them!

Now I grasp the feelings of those emotions and feel them and delight in their reality, Soul Shadows. Now I know that to experience a Soul Shadow and to know it for what it is; is to be given the opportunity of knowledge. Later my intellectual mind will know the details. For now I will use the positive quality of the Soul (Unconditional Love) to lift the shadow from my true being and later I will consciously know the content of that particular Soul Shadow.

I didn't know these possibilities back then, and so began to be darkened by many Soul Shadows; experiencing abject misery when not knowing what to do with it seemed pointless. "It's part of the process" I was told. A very long process it seemed. Simultaneously the goal posts of qualification were ever moving away over some far distant hill with the space in between filled with hours and hours of voluntary work, hours of supervision to be paid for and even more hours of personal therapy, also to be paid for. That did not come cheaply. I could see then why an hour's therapy costs so much (there was an enormous training debt to recoup) and I could see far too clearly for comfort that most people were being denied this avenue of help because of the vastness of the purse that led to it.

Meanwhile, who was dealing with the emerging Shadows? My own were definitely not the only ones; I was surrounded by gloomy trainees, some I believe quite seriously weighed down and all of us 'in the dark'. This set off alarm bells in my head and a hell of a lot of questions about myself and my motives. I could not disassociate myself with my suffering colleagues, yet had I not said that I was OK? By using others as my reflection I had to eat those words, there in front of me, beside me and around me were the illustrations. The 'ill' trying to heal themselves by healing others? The 'carers' hoping to be cared for by offering love to all? I could see it all so clearly staring me in the face. I WAS ONE OF THEM. Well, that was OK wasn't it? I mean, if you have no experience of the darker sides of life how can you possibly develop sympathy and understanding for those that are living there? With that thought I struggled on, after all I was undergoing hours of therapy and that would sort it all wouldn't it?

The doubts were growing with those things that nagged and niggled in my thoughts. Why did the girl with fourteen years in therapy have so many social problems within the group? why was another always ill and missing so many sessions? did the tutor really have to erect that unassailable wall around himself, while thrusting his physical being so laconically into our midst? and why did my therapist insist on telling me that I must, and I repeat, must,be angry? I definitely had not reached a point of anger, I'm not sure I have anger in me.

Soul Listening

Frustration, pain, fear, yes, I had plenty of that, but no-one mentioned fear then, when and where they were in the game of dealing with fear; just as no-one mentioned Soul during my spiritual quest. It's as if the simple basic roots, the uncomplicated, straightforward source of anything is constantly over looked. Is it seen as unworthy to be simple? Who has ever proved that the answer (that is, the root or source) is only a viable option if it is bizarrely complex? I was coming to the conclusion that too many things were unnecessarily complicated and involved and no proof was being offered for the things taught to me.

Unknown to my tutors I stopped having the compulsory therapy; I had convinced myself of its worthlessness, for me it was a non-starter. Years later I hear that some of my fellow students are still hooked into their sessions believing them to be necessary for their well being; I peer and still cannot see any evidence of that wellbeing, nor do I see much improvement. With hindsight I know that I made the right assessment of my situation. I was becoming more and more disillusioned.

The memory of a well qualified and experienced psychiatrist patting me on the head during one of my tearful asylum visits and emphatically telling me not to worry as "these people don't know anything" (meaning they were not feeling any of their suffering) has never left me. I was very young then and not able to express myself to this elder and therefor better (I was taught that, were you?) My words then, like the memory now, stuck in my throat, but at that tender age I knew that what he was saying was not true. At the time I was dumb, I was the unheard child, but I knew that he was wrong. Now the knowledge and experience I have validate the child's understanding.

Once again now, in the company of qualified people I was finding myself at a loss. I thought that they would be able to teach me things that were valuable, but that wasn't so. I could find no value, worse than that I was not getting any nearer to my personal truth.

Here I would like to acknowledge the good work that is done. I know some people find relief through counselling; I know some people find answers from psychotherapy; I know my own father has had small periods of relief from the torment of his mind, through drugs: yet to me these appear as rather small plasters applied to enormous wounds, at best the suppression of symptoms, never dealing with the root cause, the source, never a cure.

THIS IS GARBAGE. That's what I feel as I look back over the last few lines of yesterdays tapping. I'm searching trying to try to find out where I had got to, in order to get tapping today.

As ever the feelings that come to me when I get here, in the tappers chair, are those that are not just pertinent to the situation that I find I am in on

In search of my Soul

a daily basis, they reflect also the relevant essence of the past. Being very honest with you and myself, I was at that time of training and weekly therapy feeling far too frequently that 'this is garbage' and very definitely wondering 'where I had got to'. I felt that I was witnessing the lame holding the lame and the blind leading the blind, in my personal therapy it was the deaf hearing the dumb. You're right that's physically impossible. I felt up against the proverbial brick wall. I was enjoying the reading, theories and ideas, each trying to unravel another part of the development and workings of the human brain and mind, a subject that has always completely fascinated me. Weren't they though all trying to put across the same principles, expounding the same theories, just using different words; complex, long, convoluted, muddling and elitist in the special language of their psychologies? Weren't we all becoming blinded by the science of it? Wasn't there perhaps a simple source to all the ills of the mind, and therefor a simple solution?

It appeared not; the text-books were revered, the therapy even more so. Oh, I could see logic in the reasoning and could understand how the clinical models of treatment had been devised, but I couldn't see it working effectively. I was fascinated and repelled, both at the same time. I sensed Jung had discovered how things really might be, but my peers and superiors, who worked by his text quoting his lines and delivering his theories with great aplomb, appeared to me to be missing the point. My understanding was completely different. This was not a studied response, it was an inner knowing. I firmly believed that I understood exactly what his words meant, (and remember he had experienced the dark side of the mind so his understanding of how things might be was not theoretically based) yet I could not express that. My understanding was not in my intellectual mind. Any attempts to put my beliefs into words were useless at that time, though the inner certainty so compelled me with its voice that my uncertainties about where I was going and what I was doing, grew.

The turmoil took its toll on me; as usual at such times I became more and more under the domination of my physical being. The one that suffered chronic, worrying pelvic pain, and periodic strange ailments accompanied always by excruciatingly painful symptoms; and those black depressions that I knew and feared descended. I looked long and hard at what I was experiencing, leaving therapy sessions in a state of numbness or grief, turned out on the dot of fifty nine minutes (the therapist's hour) even if I was blinded by tears. Could that really be the way for one human being to treat another under the umbrella of care. Where was the love? Could I do that? No way. Did I want to be a person in the position to do that? Definitely not.

I looked long and hard at others who now appeared to me to be carrying all their personal discoveries in large plastic bags, no more sure what to do with their revelations than they had been when said things were hidden inside them. Worse, displaying these wares seemed to cause them more social grief than might have been felt before.

I looked long and hard at my perceived goal. It seemed even more shrouded in the mists of uncertainty; but I would battle on. Despite inner feelings of my not being in the right place I would make it come right; the negative ego had me well in its clutches still. I had to achieve that important title, without which I was 'persona non grata' and I was looking for acceptance if you remember. Yes I could march on, my mind could rationalise my decision; but my body? That had other ideas.

Well, really it was my Soul that had those other ideas, but as I was still oblivious to its voice, the only course of action for it was to throw up a few Soul Shadows in the shape of pain (physical and mental) and try to attract my attention that way. It worked, for when feeling very sorry for myself one day I remembered that a friend, from the first development circle that I ever went to, had given me the number of a "brilliant" man she had met. I had kept it for nearly two years without feeling any desire to make contact, decided it was probably another circle of people investigating spiritual happenings and I'd left that behind on my shelf of non starters.

Then suddenly I wanted to ring. I needed help, as I had done so many times in the past, so I phoned to make an appointment filled with the hope that this time I would really get it. That is how I came to find myself sitting across a room from a round, brown Tibetan. "How can I help you?" Not what I'd expected to hear. More like going to the doctor, although, on second thoughts, I was there because I was in pain, both in body and mind, which is exactly the same reasons that we have for going to the doctor. I had been there, naturally, in the past, for that pain in my abdomen. I'd been in hospital to be investigated; I'd been back, seen one specialist, and another and another, over the years. There was nothing to be found, and as the years went by and I didn't die I learnt to live with it, though not very graciously. Sometimes I howled to myself and was almost driven to plunging a knife deep inside to remove the tormenting, torturing pain. My mind was constantly occupied with the process of ignoring the nagging, continuos hurt; that didn't leave a lot of room for living. Life was a battle which I survived but never won.

Now, here was the question," how can I help you?" I don't recall what I said, there was no need to say much at all, for my pain (which was the manifestation in my body of my emotional hurts) was all too apparent. Because there was no need, there was no attempt to hide it, here with this man who people took their pain to.

One thing I recall vividly; the moment I looked at him I heard a loud inner voice say to me, "this is my teacher." I know that I didn't heed that there

In search of my Soul

and then, I was in pain, but later that day I heard it loud and clear again; I knew it was true. I can't describe the feelings that I had then, but you all know them, cloud nine, heart lifting, feet not touching the ground and so on. My anticipation for the future soared; this was what I had been looking for, for so long, my teacher. I knew there would be one; I knew that if I kept on looking, searching, eventually I would find him. I had always been convinced that there existed, somewhere, the wise person who would make sense of everything for me. He would have all the answers to those never ending questions of mine, he would know the reasons for all the things that puzzled and perplexed me, he would know what I should do to make everything come right.

I had two sessions with him, just two. In those two I learnt how I had experienced my childhood, in essence that is, for it is the emotional feelings that need to be dealt with, not the intellectual memories which have become negative mind programming. (I am always talking about the destructive events of life, as we never seek help with the positive ones!) I learnt as well, so quickly, the source of that pain I needed to exorcise.

Previously, trying to do this I had had some therapy on the NHS, which was non-effective, and then had spent a small fortune on hypnotherapy, also ineffective. No: more than that, I experienced hypnotherapy as dangerous. My last session left me with the effect of having the lid taken off my Pandora's box; crudely, but definitely descriptive of the situation I then found myself in, the scab picked off my boil. For what then erupted was a nightmare, literally. Almost every night for eighteen months or more, an hour or so after I had fallen peacefully asleep, I would wake feeling indescribably ill (something akin to food poisoning I think describes it best). It wasn't until I had endured over a year of pain, shakes, shivers and sweats (and tottering to the toilet) and discovered, once again that I hadn't died, that I realised the cause of my ills. FEAR the ruler of mind and body. Once I acknowledged that, I experienced my symptoms in a different way. They felt just the same but I could put them into a new perspective (or see them in a different light). Instead of being frightened by what was happening to me physically and instead of letting that fear fill my mind, I was able to use my mind to tell myself that what I was feeling was just the result of fear; therefor I was not feeling fear, (only the result of it.) Ergo I was not actually frightened of anything at that time. Once I was able to respond in this way, that is to experience the bodily feelings of fear, while knowing in my mind that I was not actually frightened, then, the night-terrors (as I'd come to call them) gradually went away.

Are you thinking, stupid woman, why did she go through all that, why didn't she go back to the hypnotherapist, why didn't she go to the doctor? I had long since lost confidence in the medical profession; I had lost all confidence in the effectiveness of hypnotherapy (even if I could have afforded any more of that.)

Now, as I re-live that time by telling you about it I understand that it was something I had to experience for myself. What I have come to believe in could not be learnt from books, it wasn't in any, and I probably wouldn't have believed it anyway; I have had to experience the concepts of my theories, in this case the effect of fear (negative conditioning) in the body. Now that I have 'been there myself' it is very real to me. This was one of those profound learning times; in physical terms it left an unsinkable memory, in my mind it planted an unshakeable belief. Had it not gone on for so long, long enough to become part of me, I suspect that it would have faded into those veils of disbelief that so often swathe to obscure our barely glimpsed 'revelations'. At the time though, wondering what the hell was going on, I had a very deep sense from 'inside' that it was simply something I had to experience. From that I learnt about fear and its power to transform both mind and body into wrecks. The top was off my boil and out came the puss, but at the time I didn't know the cause of that dreadful infection.

So what was the Tibetan offering me, and others? He offered himself, to be used as power (like a well-charged battery) to be used as a reflection (like a well-polished mirror) and he gave his heart. It was very effective, very quick, and only painful for a few minutes. I left smiling not sobbing, I slept soundly not troubled.

He taught his truth, his belief, that the heart, envisaged as a symbol of the individuals choosing, could be used as a personal tool for healing. He tried to teach about 'feeling the feelings' and 'facing the fears'. I say tried, for I have seen how difficult this sort of thing is. I know that I really hadn't got the foggiest idea what people were talking or reading about when I was being told to 'go with the flow', 'love yourself', 'let go', and so many more ditties. Gobbledegook! Until the time comes when you experience inner growth yourself; then you can put your own interpretation of what you have learned into words that you can understand.

I joined his group to learn more, and was surprised to find him not so round, brown and definitely not Tibetan. I had indeed seen my teacher, his also.

I didn't learn all I'd hoped to. That long-sought teacher was after all not there, but I learnt all that was right for me to learn at that time. Above all I learnt the source of my ills and was guided to a possible way of self help and self healing. This was the most precious gift any one could possibly have offered me; until then I had been hatching a loudly buzzing bee in my bonnet that healing was something that was only available to people who had unlimited funds to take them on the expensive search for it. I know life has no justice, but that had seemed too unjust and because of that not acceptable to the optimist in me.

I stayed with the group for some time and using the 'heart symbol'

In search of my Soul

(sometimes a shining gold metal ball, sometimes a white flower) I shone my own healing power onto my pain as it re-occurred. It really took no time at all to go, measured against the thirty-five years I had endured it. I felt the receiver of a miracle. For the second time in my life I had been guided to the power of my own inner resources, but I still did not know that that power came from my Soul.

Our teacher went away for some months, and five of us tried to continue the group. One evening a box of cards was brought along and we experimented with them. There were no instructions, and I was voted to 'read' them, being the "psychic one" (remember this was a group that was very much on the spiritual trail!) Reading was no problem, they spoke for themselves. In no time at all we learnt that one of us had been born no bigger than a bag of sugar, had been physically attached to her grandmother for warmth and was never expected to survive. This had left an enormous psychological debt. It was obvious that, despite very real physical survival, in her mind she had no business being alive, she was not supposed to be, and so she was living as it were on a stolen passport and working herself off her legs as a nurse; not just metaphorically speaking either, as she was suffering very painful leg ulcers which would not respond to any treatment and amputation had been muted.

See what I mean about our physical world mirroring our inner world. I found it utterly fascinating, even more so when her best friend said, somewhat indignantly, that she had never even told her any of that. My part was to assure her that she most definitely was meant to experience this life, indeed if she had not been meant to survive then undoubtedly she would not have. There is a postscript to this story. Shortly after that particular evening the lady began new treatment for her bad leg and when I next saw her, some few months later, the leg was completely healed. How we continually manage to deny the things that stare us in the eye is remarkable. I propose it is yet more proof of the view of the negative mind, the one which having been programmed by fear, distorts, clouds and confuses normal good sense.

When I started to realize just what was going on it was as if someone had walked into that dark room that was my mind and switched on a thousand watt bulb. Now I began to understand one thing we had all heard about on our spiritual quests, enlightenment. Here it was, so simple, nothing more that letting the light in, dispelling some of the gloom (negativity) that blocks the clear vision, and with a little more of the fear out of the way, the fearful mind loses a little of its power. Eureka, I began to see things clearly, the way they really are, not contorted by conditioning and not fogged by fear. "Joy of joys, I think I've got it, I'm beginning to see the light, I am becoming enlightened." Do you know what? In my appreciation of things I actually began to feel lighter and my physical being shared that feeling. It really does work on all levels.

I did not return to the group again. I was so enjoying the meetings of the five and saw great scope for us all to learn and grow but that wasn't the consensual view. Sadly we fell apart and I was reminded of the families who fall out after a matriarchal figure has departed; the leadership goes and quarrelling over asset sharing disrupts.

Once more I was back on the open road, looking for new signposts. There was nothing to be seen anywhere!
I was reminded of something recently talked about; it had cropped up at New Year. Asked at the group what we hoped for in the next year the responses mostly began with "I want......." which was a good opportunity to be reminded by our teacher that wanting encourages want as needing encourages need. We looked at just being. This is something touched on many times, but extremely difficult to achieve if you are not told what it is. I had no idea what it meant.
Now I remembered this and made a conscious decision to spend my time just being. So now, planning just being for at least the foreseeable future, I was struck by the memory of my own hopes for that coming year. I could still hear my voice saying that I was going to find myself. Could there be a way to achieve this? Could I find myself by being; not wanting, needing, wishing, or hoping? It should be possible, after all we are human beings, not human doings (although most of us act like this) not human wantings (although we all do this too much of the time) nor human needings (though goodness me, when did you last see a person not in need). The more I thought about it, the more convinced I became that to 'just be' could be the solution to my problems. It was hard, stopping all that flapping about, chasing ideas, dreaming up schemes, raising challenges. In a way it felt like giving up on life. To quietly be, doing only what was to be done, not looking about for all those things I could be doing.
The cosmos helped me. I'd tried to get a part-time job (many times) without success, one way or another all the interests and pass-times that I have pursued over the years had gone from my life. My last child had started prep school with long hours away from home, my daughter's new job took her away from the house for longer days and my eldest son had finally left the nest. I had never before been so little in demand. My life had never before had so little in it. There it was around me with nothing much more than me in it. Now was surely the right time to make an all out effort at this 'being' lark.
What did being mean? BEING *existing, nature, essence*. I didn't know my essence, was unsure of my nature, and hadn't learned to exist in comfort. I hadn't learnt how to be, so I set to then. The result was that I was able to hear myself much more easily. In fact that's mostly what I did hear,

myself. It wasn't nice. I found it very uncomfortable, because the only way I could hear myself was through my discomforts. These were those physical and mental 'sounds' I've told you a little about, the ones that we normally brush aside, battle with, or seek medical help with. Not only could I hear them now but I discovered that I wanted to listen.

At long last I was beginning to hear my Soul talking to me as it shook off another of its Shadows for me to experience and deal with. That's what I did, each and every time I didn't feel quite right. First I experienced EXPERIENCE *meet with, feel, undergo* and EXPERIENCE *actual observation of, practical acquaintance with facts or event.* As the definitions imply, I observed, using my brain, every detail of the feeling or feelings that I was undergoing. I gained a practical acquaintance, therefore knowledge of those feelings. Was it a pain? an ache? a prick? a wound? a cut? a break? Was I bruised? broken? crushed? I used my brain to observe all the minute details of my feelings, and then used it some more to meet with, undergo and feel. In exactly the same ways as the word is defined, so I experienced my feelings, and I did this with my brain, a clear, sharp, bright, focused brain.

Then I dealt with the feelings. DEAL *distribute, give out, deliver as share or deserts to person.* True again to the definition I gave out to my person my deserts. DESERTS *deserving, being worthy of reward.* I had learnt about the power of the heart symbol and now I would test it. Without the presence of the catalyst for healing (my former teacher) I would invoke my own inner power and now we would see whether there really was anything in it. So I visualised my personal symbol and willed it to 'shine' me well, 'shine' me whole, 'shine' all those symptoms away. IT WORKED. When I dealt with the negative feelings in that way, I got my deserts, the reward I deserved.

Something was really happening now, and it was something that I, in my wildest dreams and my soaring imaginings, had never begun to touch on. There I was, just being (well, trying to) and there it was, (in the midst of my trying) it was there. There was no searching, no bidding or calling, it just was and is if I just BE. So I discovered the real meaning of being (look back please). As the dictionary states, nature, essence. I was finding my essence. ESSENCE *all that makes a thing what it is, intrinsic nature.* I was beginning to discover the intrinsic nature of being, and, though unknown to me then, I was just stepping onto the path that would lead to my discovering (in my truth) the intrinsic nature of being human. HUMAN *of or belonging to the genus homo, distinguished from animals by superior mental development, power of articulate speech and upright posture.* Hmmmph! I don't think any of that says much to me. INTRINSIC *belonging, inherent, essential.* That says so much more.

Can my ego have a look in here? I so wish I was a real writer, not for any glory, not for the dough, no. What I could do if I was a writer would be to put some magic into these words, to give them life of their own; with that magic and life they would conjure for you the things that were then going through my mind. How can I ever paint things as bright and exciting as they appeared? So many things were buzzing in my head, it seemed as though there were no end to the possibilities for and of everything. On a daily basis I really was feeling enlightened, I felt sure that I was seeing so many things anew and I was. There was light and understanding tumbling into those dark corners of my mind and there was light falling into the hidden, neglected corners of my body. I had to work at it and I was tested, but slowly and surely many, many things gained a new perspective and my symptoms were disappearing.

One of the notable things that happened concerned my father. His mental problems have got worse with old age, for a few years now I have not been able to cope with all the difficulties he brings. Is that true? No. The truth is that I have not wanted to cope with the problems, it has all become too much for me.

I used to have him to stay every other weekend and at high days and holidays. There was a time when his medication kept him almost 'socially' acceptable, and he enjoyed our farm life and the fishing there, and we could laugh with him at any idiosyncracies. The children found him a constant source of fun. But medication has many downsides and when the complications of senility, incontinence and lost mobility weighed on the already troubled dear, well, in truth, I just couldn't bear the weight of grief, helplessness and guilt that I felt. 'Out of sight out of mind.' Sadly there's a deal of truth in that. Out of sight is a very good way to shelve those really hard pressing problems.

When my father became less able to travel under his own steam (and steam he certainly had) I didn't collect him as often as he would have enjoyed. One day, in his late seventies, he decided that he wanted to come 'home' to the farm here that is. Some things are so simple in the disturbed mind; he wanted to be here, so off he set to walk from his care-home to mine, all fourteen miles along a busy main road, not much in the way of pavements and plenty of dual carriage way with the speeding traffic that that brings. No money in his pockets, no provision for any change in the weather, no provision for the 'inner man' to sustain him on his journey. He just wanted to come home, so he did, coming in style for the last two miles in a police car. He wasn't tired, or particularly hungry, nor, most interestingly to me, was he in the least bit agitated or frightened by something which many people in their 'right' mind would have perceived, at the very least, as daunting. It was perfectly natural to him to pursue what he wanted, to take charge, find his own strength to do for himself something that he desired, something that he knew would not be done for him.

We were all amazed by his capacity to find the way and the strength. I was reminded at the time of other instances of the hidden power that so-called mental illness can release. Or, does it give access to? A tremendous physical power that seems to be unleashed by thought; unfortunately it seems to be the negative thoughts that trigger the greatest physical power and disaster is too often a consequence: in this instance though all had a happy ending.

I was finding my visits to him were not as frequent as I felt that they should be. Each time I saw him he wanted to know if I was taking him home; usually this meant he had mistaken me for my mother. At times like that I quickly learnt to keep hold of his hands which could fly to my throat with the speed of light. The first time that happened I was bending over him in hospital after he had broken his hip. I managed to release myself, but the shock left my body quaking and my mind reeling. It was a new experience of him and really put the wind up me; since that I'm always alert to this possibility, which adds a different dimension to our relationship altogether. It saddens me that I am no longer completely at ease with him, but it served me a vital lesson.

I know that I experienced for a brief time the terrifying uncertainty that, for a while, was the life my mother knew with him. That put a new perspective on my understanding of her as I was able to accept what I had been harbouring deep inside. As a child, an onlooker at the parental relationship, I know that I had judged her harshly for 'getting rid' of him. Oh, not consciously, not overtly, but I can now almost feel the vow I was making inside then; avowing the knowledge (it seemed that, then) that if I were in her shoes, then absolutely no way would I not be willing to keep such a sick and troubled man in my care, no way would I put him away.

Such are the powerful energies of the cosmos that I was invited to 'put my money where my mouth was' and repeat her experience when I found myself in the position of wife of a disturbed and violent man. I tried long and hard to succeed where I judged that she had failed, and I failed too, and it was nearly fatal. It was a long time before I began to see the same pattern had repeated itself. I had to wait for the contact with my Soul before a glimmering of understanding began to penetrate that particular fog. Perhaps that's why it was only relatively recently that I experienced my father's attempts at strangulation, any sooner and they would have been wasted as a means of enlightenment; worse, I might have given up on him out of fear. I believe I was able to experience my father's first attack on me in the way my mother had hers, to feel how she felt and to know, really know, the sensations of her emotions. When I had been through that, all the judgements that I had made of her evaporated. I knew that she had done what she had to do for her perceived survival and at last I respected that. I told her how I felt, but I don't think she had any idea what I was really talking about.

That's one more lesson I've learnt, I can change myself, but never get the gratification of changing any one else. I find that a hard one. I convince myself (wrongly) that the change I hope for in others is for their good, what I forget is that change comes from within and is therefor personal property, I have no right to expect change from others. It took me seventeen years to accept that I could not change (help) my husband and another seventeen to learn to respect the individual's choice to be how they want to be.

It is not that any of us refuse change, (development) it is that until we see things in a fresh light we do not even know of its existence. I was seeking enlightenment (change, development) so I must have believed in its existence, nevertheless it was not in any way real to me and so I could not find it. Then suddenly it found me. I think that is how it is; it definitely cannot be taught or sought in others, but if you are patient and prepared to spend time 'being', then it finds you, as it found me.

Perhaps you have understood something of the distress that visiting my father caused me. Whether he recognised me as myself (his only child) or perceived me as my mother both scenarios caused him great pain and anguish and rarely was a visit without tears, never without his pleas to "take me home with you." I had been finding all this and the worsening of his physical and mental condition (rocking and agitated by the permanent state of fear he was in) too hard to witness. I also left in tears each time, feeling as though I had been ripped apart inside. Imagine my joy then when I begun to experience a change in my reaction to him; I suddenly found that the dreadful emotional trauma I went through after each visit was not occurring. Nothing at all was different about him, I still thought the same way about his sufferings yet I was not being drawn into them with him. Although I could feel his pain and know his fear, none of it touched me at the level where it hurt. The negative energies that had bound us together were no longer there, the 'hooks' we have which keep us on the merry-go-round of our negative conditioning had gone.

By using my heart symbol as I had been shown (visualising the symbol shining light to the area of my body affected) a change had come about in me. Although the situation with my father was unchanged, that is, he remained as sick as always, I was no longer carrying his pain, as my if it were my own; there was no longer anything in me for it to hook onto or into. It seemed that I had gained a totally new perspective of the situation, somewhere there had been a change in my understanding.

Anyone looking in from the outside would have seen nothing different, father just as sick, daughter looking as usual. That was from the outside, from the inside I was different, but I guess that could only have been seen by someone with developed Soul contact. Inside I was healed, freed of the negative conditioning, the fear, things that make up these hooks I talk of. With those gone, however my father presented himself to me, there was nothing in me that could now receive the hurt in the previously self-destructive way; no hooks left to catch it on.

In search of my Soul

I thought then that I had really understood the nature of enlightenment. I had changed some previously (subconsciously) held belief and from that I had come to experience a very familiar life-long situation in a completely new way and to view it in a totally different light. Outwardly, worldly, nothing was altered, but in the experience of my being, inwardly, every about this situation was different. My emotions were no longer being mangled, which made me feel physically lighter. ENLIGHTEN *free (person) from prejudice or superstition*. I think that says as much as I am managing to in the way of conveying how I understood enlightenment from then on. It was truly a feeling of freedom, and if you can accept 'prejudice' as negative mind conditioning (fear), I can state that, from then on, I was free of that particular prejudice. Since that day I visit my father confident that I will not experience the emotion of his pain, but confident also that I am just as able to empathise with him as I ever was. From my being the situation is healthy, and that is what enlightenment leads to, health. HEALTH *soundness of body or mind*, SOUND *healthy, not diseased or injured or rotten*. I like to think that in this area of my being I am no longer diseased, injured or rotten. I most definitely was before.

I am reminded now, as I search the dictionary to share the understanding of my words, of how my father, during many of his worst psychotic episodes, would 'play' with words. In doing that he was, I'm certain, describing his altered perspective, his own enlightenment. I watched how the effect of this perceived new understanding of our language gave him joy and excitement; perhaps at those times he also experienced some freedom from prejudice (understood as above.) I look at the word 'healthy' and find myself pronouncing it heal thy. I like that way of knowing the word, after all wasn't I talking of enlightenment and trying to describe to you, how to me that was beginning to mean better health, healthy relationships. That's what my father might have written, heal thy. HEAL *restore*, THY *of thee*, THEE *see* THOU, THOU poss. THY, THINE, THINE *mine*. I believe I am thinking how he was thinking.

I recall being fascinated by the proposals he made when he was playing with words, many times there seemed some rationale to his games. By splitting and then spelling parts of the word in the way they sounded to him he would propose things, in this altered language, that really did offer an alternative explanation. Doing that gave a completely new understanding of whatever word had captured his imagination. Very often this different view of things familiar was acceptable, even enlightening, most often amusing, and I probably humoured his efforts. You see, he was mentally ill, wasn't he? These were the ramblings of a demented mind, weren't they? Part of me accepted that way back then, for the experts had told me so, but as I look back now I know that I felt curious. I wasn't able to completely write off those wordy insights; now I am certain that he had tapped into something important with his 'demented mind of the mentally ill'.

I am proposing to you in all seriousness that we can look at the words we use and find another layer of meaning in them. It seems to me that all things physical have layers (at this moment I'm not sure how many) and that each layer (or side, or aspect) is a different view of the same thing. Each view offers a different understanding. Perhaps if we could find all the aspects, see all the views, we could gather a comprehensive picture and from that gain complete understanding through knowledge of the broader spectrum. However, on the whole we see only one or perhaps at best two sides to everything.

Perhaps you don't agree that there is more to see, or maybe you think there is but have no idea how to access it. ACCESS *right or means of reaching.* The right to look for those other layers, or should I be saying dimensions, is one's own. The right is easily owned when fear has been banished. The means of reaching is listening, from the Soul, when fear has been banished from the mind. I saw the word healthy given as the outcome of enlightenment, I listened and heard HEAL THY, and I understand this to mean restore mine. MINE me. Thus RESTORE ME! I am uplifted now! As I see that before me I am almost in tears of joy for I know that I am being restored each day I work with Soul. This Soul is mine, for the benefit of me, for my health, for my own healing.

This is not a selfish proposition. You have one also, exclusive to you, for your own health and your own healing. All Souls are joined as a great Cosmic Soul. The use of your own, for you, has a huge knock on effect. As you use yours the universal energy of Unconditional Love is invoked and an automatic link is forged between Souls, through this link flows the Unconditional Love from the universe. You cannot use your Soul without this process taking place, (the flow of Unconditional Love that is) and in flowing it touches all Souls and restores the Soul's power. It requires nothing more than acknowledgement, knowing you have a Soul, knowing it is your power centre and knowing that the power it offers is that of Unconditional Love. THAT CAN MOVE MOUNTAINS.

No wonder my Dad played his word games in his deepest insanity, he was just being himself at that time and it restored him.

Gradually in my time of just being and listening to myself I was being restored. RESTORE *(attempt) to bring back to original state by rebuilding, repairing; emending.* I had declared that I was going to find myself and there I was working to bring myself to my original state. ORIGINAL *innate, existing from the first.* The dictionary kindly, or wisely, bracketed attempt. It was definitely an attempt as I was still working largely with my mind which, conditioned by much negativity, had no idea of my innate state. Such a mind definitely would not have passed on that sort of classified information, handing over that power would surely have led to its downfall!

Unknown to me at the time, when I had confidently stated that during the coming year my intention was to 'find myself', I must have heard the voice of my Soul, I must have given a chink of space in my life to be able to hear that voice. The surprise is that I had not heard it before, it certainly shouts loud enough to be heard.

How does it do that you might ask? I believe that everything that happens to us in our lives, those overlooked incidents, like a flat tyre on the way to something important, an illness which stops us doing something we really want to, an accident of any sort, and so on and so on ad infinitum, have purpose. I suggest that every thing about us which trips us up, metaphorically and literally, is the visible outer, physical, life reflection of our inner life. Inner life in this context is all things that hold us back; the negative mind-set of our childhood conditioning. We all have some; no-one is exempt, though the degree of difficulty we are presented with in our individual lives varies. It doesn't always follow that the deepest traumas lead to the deepest problems; I have been surprised sometimes by the incongruities I've seen. Things which may not seem at all dramatic or traumatic to one person can have a more profound effect on another than one could imagine possible even for a holocaust victim. This suggests to me that the Soul is indeed immortal, bringing with it to each new existence the Soul Shadows of previous life experiences. For me, thus far, I have found no better explanation for the incongruities, and so that is what I accept as my truth. I am certain that I have 'been here' before, but for the purpose of my story it doesn't feel necessary even to ask you whether you believe in reincarnation or whether you think it's hog-wash (you may be reminded here that I was a farmer's wife.)

As I said before, there appear to be so many layers, so many sides or aspects to everything that in some cases I may talk about views which you have not yet experienced, knowing while I'm doing this that you will more than likely have a perspective that I've not yet seen. But it was a long time before I realised that I only had to look around me to understand, to be enlightened about the things that ailed me. Using the physical life is a quick way to understanding the possibilities of a spiritual life, but it's part of a process that for me only offered its clarity after a lot of hard work.

Isn't that what we were told? Nothing worthwhile is gained without toil. Hard work reaps its rewards. No wonder we find beginning the journey almost too difficult, it certainly feels a lot easier and definitely far more comfortable to remain where we are. Isn't life hard work enough already without knowingly letting ourselves in for another basinful?

Soul Listening

I had taken that decision though, and was working hard. It was hard, truly, and painful a lot of the time. Many times my mind almost convinced me that I was not getting anywhere, physical and mental relapses had me almost believing what my mind kept telling me. I almost gave the work up, almost, never quite, despite my misgivings, and there were many of those.

For one thing I found it hard to accept that this path to better things should be so damn difficult, it seemed to be doing it's utmost to keep people off it. Was there any reason why it was such hard work? Was that really logical? Then there was again the voice of the negative mind, trying to convince me of the improbability of succeeding, asking could I really follow this route I could only see somewhere within? Thank goodness the power within kept finding what it took to keep me from falling by the wayside, from turning deaf ears to its voice.

It didn't all come from inside, it never does, there has to be harmony and balance between all things to maintain a flow. The great cosmos aided my search for 'self' and my attempts 'to be' by keeping people away from me. At first I was overjoyed to find myself free of some of my family commitments and to have the house to myself, but something very weird was happening and for months hardly anyone visited and almost no-one responded to my letters or left messages.

I was alone, and feeling lonely and alone. ALONE *not with others, standing by oneself.* LONELY *solitary, isolated, companionless, unfrequented.* Looking back I think it was truly the first time that I was 'standing by myself' (in every sense of the word that you can imagine) and I felt solitary and isolated. So I worked with that. They were after all my own accepted and acceptable emotions being reflected in the life I was leading then. They showed how things had been 'inside' for me sometimes in my life and highlighted some of the negative mind conditioning of my formative years. So I used the 'heart symbol' technique, which led to understanding within my mind and exorcism of the bad feelings from wherever they emanated. I have said heart symbol here, on purpose, for at that time my Soul, although working overtime to be heard, had not made itself known to me. That was to come, very soon.

We had supper with old school friends during this time, after which I was thinking what small gift I could give the cook. Searching my grey matter I was reminded of a surprising fact that had come to light during the evening. The 'cooks' husband, a former barrister had developed an interest in Tarot cards and was collecting different sets from around the world as he travelled on business. He was the last person that I would have imagined I would be hearing this from and the surprise had lodged in my mind. Not surprising then I suppose that I should recall some cards from America that I had seen in my group some six months before; although I had not given them a thought from that day to

41

In search of my Soul

this. I'd got it; a pack of those cards would make an ideal gift, easy. Easy it was not. No shop could be found that had even heard of them. The owner of the original pack had given them to her daughter and they could not be found. I gave up on that idea and penned a thank you rhyme instead. But the idea of such a gift nagged away.

Some months later the pack of cards was found, not as permanently hidden as had been thought. In fact they came to light right under their owner's nose sitting quite visibly in a much used drawer. Although they now had no box or instructions she was confident that they were called Soulcards and the sight of them sent me off anew to find a pack for my host.

At exactly this time my daughter, wandering about in her lunch hour, discovered a 'New Age' shop and came home full of talk about all the crystals, cards, books, tapes etc. that she had been looking at. A few days later I found myself in the area and went in to ask whether they had any Soulcards. "Soulcards? No. What are they?" However the girl behind the counter was also the shop owner and looked in her supplier's catalogue. Not listed there. She persevered and phoned said supplier. I could hardly believe it as she mouthed through a smile, "They've just walked through the door; do you want some?" She ordered two packs and said they'd be in in a few days time. I came home very excited that at last I would be able to express my appreciation of my friends hospitality (I'm no good at reciprocating that sort of invite as I don't like cooking at the best of times and it weighs heavy when I have to do it for others.)

So some days later found me back at the shop to collect the cards. One thing about the shop which I forgot to mention was that it was also a therapy centre and offered meditation, workshops and 'readings' of various sorts. I took my pack of cards, handed over a note and waited for the change. As it was given to me the girl said, "Would you like to be a reader, we need another one?" Knock me down with a feather. I'd set out to buy a gift for a friend. I'd left all this new age stuff behind. I'd been on the receiving end of ill-advised 'readings' and vowed that whatever gift for divvying I might possess I would never go down the route of offering my insights to others. Yet now what was I hearing? That was the most important thing at that moment. What was I hearing? I probably only had a few seconds to reply. I didn't know her, she didn't know me, yet out of the blue, out of my search for that gift for my friend was the opportunity of a part-time job. Hadn't I been unsuccessfully trying to find some work? Hadn't I been studying in order to have some work? More important, wasn't I feeling alone? The answer to the last three questions was a definite YES. So I did it. I went for it, I said "OK fine, love to, when do you want me to start?" My friend? He never did get that pack of cards.

Episode Two
Going with Soul

I drove home in a mixture of emotions, part excitement and elation, part panic and uncertainty. What had I done now? What was I getting or letting myself in for? Card reading? I'd denied the Mystic Mog bit, decried it as bunkum, declared it a dangerous ego trip, yet, in the face of all that I'd accepted the invitation. Why? Just why, was the burning question as I carried the much sought after Soulcards back home. Was I Barmy Beth or was there something to be heard? Had I been listening and heard something important or was my imagination running amok again? No; I decided that there had been too many uncanny twists and turns to this event, too many surprises, too many things that could not possibly have been directed by my negative mind, after all, in the beginning the search for the cards was born out of love, almost Unconditional Love, which I was trying to express through the gift. So I made the decision to trust, to trust my instinctive split-second response, to trust that I had heard something calling me to listen.

Trust in what? Myself?

This part, the trusting myself bit, strangely could only be done by placing complete trust in the unknown, those unknown energies that devise the 'happenings' in our lives? I acknowledge them then; I acknowledged them both outwardly and inwardly and confirmed that acknowledgement by trusting both myself in my surprising decision and the universe in the road that lay ahead. I had not the foggiest notion what that might be, but as confirmation of the trust I was placing in that way ahead, I decided not to study the cards. I took off the cellophane so they were ready, I shuffled through the images, to remind myself of the beauty I recalled from the first time I saw them, and I skimmed the accompanying booklet on how they might be used, to read only their genesis.

I liked that word, and I warmed further when I read how the images had been created by an artist when she cleaned ink from her plates with paper. It seemed that the simple practical mopping up at the end of her perceived creative work as an artist was producing creations from somewhere else. Over a period of ten years she pursued her idea that images and pictures were being drawn out of her, drawn from her Soul in fact. Years later she sat next to a tarot card reader on a flight, (unknown to her he was scheduled to give her the sack at a meeting they were both flying to) a disillusioned reader, who had given that part of his life up. They got talking, she happened to have some copies of some of the, what she calls Touch Drawing images, and to cut a long story short, he took them, did a lot of readings with them, found their inspiration deep and effective and some time after Soulcards were born.

I loved the story, the twists and turns of so-called fate that I know as the gently directing energies of cosmic Unconditional Love. Everything felt right after that. The cards had no numbers, no specific meanings, and learning that from the booklet simply confirmed my belief that I was to go to the shop in total trust, without 'playing' with the cards previously. Whatever the reason they had been given to me would be made clear and I would know how I was to use them.

Once again that light-bulb flash of enlightenment went off in my head. You see the ego part of my mind had started to panic and pester me with all those self doubts about my ability to perform, be up to the mark at the right time etc.; part of me had been surprised when I heard myself calmly announcing that I was going to offer myself for public scrutiny, even failure and therefor criticism, and I was going to offer myself in complete ignorance of the circumstances, and I wasn't afraid as I had found trust. At long last I was beginning to listen to the voice of my Soul.

Have I spelt out my interest in 'mental illness' or only some of my experiences with it? Did I tell you that one of my unspoken dreams was to find the cause of that particular avenue of suffering, and then the cure? I probably haven't recounted each and every path I took to try to learn about such aberrations of the mind, but believe me when I tell you that they were many. However, my spell of psychodynamic training and my failure to find answers in all the studying there was my last attempt at understanding what, I finally came to conclude, was something beyond my comprehension. After all, more learned men than I had not really made much headway in the understanding of the human mind.

Not really surprising when you consider that most knowledge of the body has been gained from dissection and study of live parts and their functions; none of which is possible with the brain. Many studies have given us insights into our brains and some probabilities for the workings of the mind, but I felt that we were as far removed from understanding the cause and therefore the treatment of the 'mentally ill' as our forbears were hundreds of years ago. I think I finally lost heart and decided that there were not going to be any answers for me when I was taught about depression. It has been common policy to prescribe anti-depressants to inhibit some chemical imbalances discovered in the brains of people suffering from depression. Hey presto, balance the chemicals, banish the depression. Except that it doesn't always work. Hadn't

Soul Listening

my own mother got addicted to the pills? No improvement, only addiction! It seemed to me that it didn't work far too often for it to be called a cure. Do abnormal chemical levels cause depression or are they the result of a person becoming depressed? Well, obviously clinicians believed the former, but with no proof of that I was not convinced of this 'chicken and egg' situation, studies proving this and that theory seemed all too conveniently accepted. What if the depression came first, what was causing it then?

Then there was the diagnostic manual of mental disorders, yards of it; was it really possible in a field of so much uncertainty and speculation to define and divide the symptoms of a tormented mind into these neat categories, in order to label and then treat? No, I was in a dark wood here, and couldn't see that anyone I was coming into contact with had any more answers than I did. I turned my back and gave this endeavour up. I stopped searching and I stopped puzzling. I was not after all going to be the person who at long last discovers the truth about the disordered mind.

So, with that background, can you imagine my thoughts when the first customer in my 'readers' booth, having spent only a few minutes in the company of myself and my newly acquired Soulcards, pushed her clothing up to her elbows to reveal mutilated forearms? Here I was, thinking I was treading a new pathway, doing a bit of divvying, for a pound or two, in the tarot slot and here in front of me my first client in mental anguish, confronting me with my past.

Now my tapping has dried up, again. I know what I have to do, so waste no time and look to see where I am being stopped. Confronting. Surprise, that would seem a word that anyone would understand, nonetheless I do this with trust. CONFRONT *meet and look at, stand facing; be opposite to; face in hostility or defiance; bring (person) face to face.* All those things happened in that instant of her actions, and I was indeed face to face with something that I didn't understand right at that moment.

After a long session (there was no one else waiting) she told me that I had been no help to her, no help at all; in fact I had only told her what she already knew. My response to that was that I couldn't possibly take her money under such circumstances; but she insisted. I showed her to the shop door and she looked at me and smiled. It was not until I was driving home that I had chance to look at my racing thoughts and relive my shock. Why, oh why had this happened? Why had someone so disturbed come to see me? The first person over my new threshold, not only facing me with the thing I had decided to put firmly behind me, but telling me I was useless; an outright ego attack.

Do you know that only rocked me very slightly and on seeing that, I knew I had made great strides in the right direction, so I trusted the process, did my 'work' and enlightenment quickly followed. I recalled then how cowed and sad a person had come into the shop (she didn't even look at me) and I saw again the upright smiling girl who had looked directly into my eyes as she said "good-bye." Those were the important details; that is what needed to be remembered, that was all I should be thinking about. I had done my best, offered Unconditional Love, worked in complete trust and something had happened. Something positive and good had come out of our meeting. That was all that really mattered, and in seeing that and letting go of my ego's need to understand 'what I'd done', once again enlightenment followed hot-foot.

Her words that "you have only told me what I already know" held deep significance. On the face of that one would believe that nothing new had been suggested to her, but at that moment I could clearly recall her words as we talked, and the things she was telling me were almost opposite to the things the cards gave me to tell her. So, why had she said what she did? Was she lying? Definitely not, she was stating her belief, her truth; what she said as she left was the truth that came from her Soul. I don't know if she consciously heard what her Soul was telling her but I like to think her smiling face showed that she had heard, some-where. I don't know if I heard what her Soul was saying to us both then, this was just the beginning for me and my unbalanced ego still held court. Later when new light dawned I knew definitely that I had heard the voice of her Soul.

The next week when I went to the shop my name was chalked on the board in the shop doorway and the girl who owned the shop said, "Shall I put Tarot Reader?" "No" I said, "It's called Soul Listening, please put that." "Are you sure?" she said. "Oh yes, definitely, Soul Listening." No-one came in that day for me!

In the weeks that followed there was a very noticeable shortage of custom and the disappearance of the therapists was disconcerting. I felt this was a sinking ship. I only saw a handful of people, which I wasn't going to take as a personal insult; remember I was, and still am, working hard to place my ego in balance and use it in its true place. The more I trusted whatever was happening the more obvious it was to me that the work those Soulcards had instigated was not appropriate for the space and place allotted to 'readers'. I was learning fast and being led by the ring in my nose, well, that's what it felt like when my second visitor came. Talk about having said nose rubbed in it.

A sweet young girl sat opposite me, yet I was very puzzled by the cards she drew and put out on the table, they seemed totally inappropriate. My puzzlement was short-lived, as I quickly discovered that she suffered with schizophrenia (the thing I had grown up with as the reason for my father's disappearance.) I could not help wondering what the hell was going on, this was too cruelly close to home. I couldn't possibly help this young person, just as I couldn't help my father, everyone knows there is little hope for real treatment in such cases, treatment that leads to the sufferer enjoying a 'normal' existence. Hadn't I had enough experiences to know that? Hadn't I pursued the avenue of learning and found no answers to my quest? Hadn't I finally, at long last reluctantly turned my back on my hopes for solutions and my dreams of answers?

So I said again (to myself of course) "what the hell is going on." You may think there is too much use of a certain word here, but it kept feeding into my mind; hell, for that is what mental suffering produces, a kind of living hell. I know that, I've had my own times, and I've shared (too) many more times with those nearest and dearest. I thought I'd shaken it all off, decided to leave it all behind. Obviously the decision I'd made wasn't enough, or was it? Driving home on that particular day the mind was, as usual, pumping overtime. The negative mind (the ego, in unhelpful over-drive) was looping the loop, doing backflips and stomach churning diving somersaults, until I remembered to contact my Soul. That did the trick. When I stopped trying to work things out, when I let go the need for intellectual understanding, then I found the confidence to trust in the wisdom of my Soul, to tune into that, acknowledge that, and continue my journey home with a quiet, peaceful mind whose only occupation was to give all concentration to linking with the powerful, healing, Unconditional Love energy that is unique to the Soul.

You may notice that a slow but definite process was beginning to establish itself as part of my functioning. I was learning that my Soul was a very real thing, not just a word. I found that realisation slightly amusing. The fact that Soul was a word not totally alien to my previous existence, in fact quite well used in phrases like, 'Bless my soul', and the much uttered, 'Poor little soul'. Yet I used it then with no thought at all, definitely no thought as to its meaning, and never the thought that Soul was something that actually existed; never that I had a Soul in that real sense that one has lungs, liver or heart.

That sets off a new chain of thought. Heart. You recall me telling you of the heart symbol work and how effective I found it? It struck me very quickly when the Soulcards came into my life that it was not the heart that offered any solutions for healing, neither could the heart be the source of love. The heart is after all an organ, made of muscle and filled with blood, a practical vital power-house I grant you, but at the end of the day a physical part of the human body with not really a lot more significance than say lungs or liver: which is just what I was saying to myself, when the idea took hold. I had to laugh at the notion of a spiritual development group sitting in deep concentration over kidney symbols and light rays of healing love coming from the liver, it looked so comical in my minds eye, it didn't have quite the same ring of plausibility. Why not? What really differentiates those organs from the heart organ? I concluded that it had to be the idea of love, the importance we human beings heap on the ideals of love, and the association we have given love with the heart, (though I don't know how that came about.) My new notions were gathering apace, I thought about the people I had seen using 'heart methods'. What were they really doing? Certainly encouraging trust, faith in the possibility of something that each and every one of us possesses, showing a way to self help and self healing; but what made it work? (when it did.) It seems to me that one thing was the key, love. But what is love?

I needed to define that, and thinking of what I've tapped here I know that at the moment of feeling that need I heard a voice shouting for my attention, NEED. I decided there and then that my understanding of human love is something that is based on need; I dare to say that it is need. The biological need to continue the species, the physical need to be fed, the emotional need to be cared for and the psychological need to share our lives journeys. Every aspect of those things that I mulled over seemed to have possible overtones of selfishness and I could not see love in any light but that of seeking to satisfy very complex and convoluted human drives (for that substitute needs.)

Yet I had seen the power of love at work. There had to be something else. In me, then, was the birth of the notion of Unconditional Love as a very different kind of love, not just a qualitative understanding of the same familiar word but a new type of love with a totally different meaning. UNCONDITIONAL *not subject to conditions*, CONDITIONS (loads to choose from here, so I'll go for the first) *stipulation, thing upon the fulfilment of which depends that of another*. That says it all doesn't it? We know love cannot really be a feeling from the heart; feelings are produced by the brain in our minds and bodies. I know that every human being has to some degree a negatively conditioned mind, the normal and natural product of our rearing, so how can anyone possibly give Unconditional Love?

Yet I believed that I had witnessed such a thing in my lifetime, I believed I had seen the effect of it, I believed in it, so where was it coming from? There was only one possible source, as far as I could see it had to emanate from the Soul. The more I thought about it the more I was convinced, those supposed 'heart symbols' they were Soul symbols no less; by visualising something, anything from which healing light could come, I and others had been summoning the power of our Souls. It seemed so obvious now.

One day I had found myself sitting, with a group of his followers, around someone from Canada who was over here to promote his having found THE TRUTH. I couldn't understand his literature. That was no surprise to me, thinking as I do that our way of communication through words is fraught with misunderstandings; I think that personal translation of words is born of individual conditioning which in turn leads to unique meanings and understandings. His way of having people sit around him and inviting them one at a time to gaze into his eyes perplexed me. I remember thinking how can he be telling any one about finding THE TRUTH when he says nothing? As well as thinking I was watching and what I saw was one after another either bursting into tears or coming out with verbal streams of anguish and turmoil. Still the man said nowt, just kept his eyes on the individual with the invitation to that person to go on looking. In? Yes, that was it, I decided. My truth about his truth was that he also had discovered some of the power of the Soul, though I'm sure he didn't know it, he certainly never mentioned it. He seriously believed that he was privy to THE TRUTH, and as you know my belief is that we all own our own individual portions of THE TRUTH and the whole therefor cannot be known by any one person. It will take complete unity of mankind, putting all those little (perhaps sometimes larger) pieces of truth together in order for us to get to THE TRUTH. Well, that's how I see it; that is my truth speaking; so you can imagine that I was somewhat cynical about his claims. Can one be cynical while holding the belief and standing by it, that everyone has the right to say and do whatever they please, as long as it harms no-one? I hope so.

I was quite excited driving home for I felt that my growing ideas about the Soul were being confirmed to me. After all hadn't I always been told that 'the eyes are the windows of the soul' and what had I just witnessed? Well, I was uncertain about that on a wide canvas, but I was utterly convinced that those 'windows of the soul' had been opened wide enough to enable a two way Soul contact which was drawing something up from the depths. Once that contact has been made there is no way that the Unconditional Love energy of the Soul can be kept in. I hadn't seen the after effects of these Soul 'touchings' but I guessed (and at that stage in my ignorance I hoped) that each one who had gazed was enjoying the beneficial results. I was quite conscious in my mind that I was thinking kindly of this man who had aroused my cynicism, and I was pleased. Pleased with myself for this acceptance; this was very much how I wanted to know myself, tolerant and open- minded.

Suddenly I realised that I was finding something to like in myself, it felt good and I bubbled. I was finding more of myself, knowing and understanding the real me, the potential of the Soul me and I liked it. I believed at that moment I finally knew what people meant when they wrote 'love yourself'. How that had annoyed me in the past, all those silly circle platitudes; they meant absolutely nothing to me then. I used to feel annoyed by the banality as they were banded about as the way forward, the things that all the developing enlightened ones did. I was definitely out on a limb, I really didn't understand any of them; they held no reality for me.

But now I did understand the true meaning of loving myself because I was beginning to do just that. It was my Soul that had guided me to that place.

I state categorically, yes vehemently, that my brain alone would never in a million years have taken me there, and my negatively conditioned mind had been doing its darndest to take me out of earshot of that gentle loving voice of my Soul. As I thought these kind and loving thoughts about myself and others, insight, enlightenment struck again.

I could hear the schizophrenic girl telling me firmly that she really did not understand how and why she was capable of so much love, when her heart was so raw. Confirmation to my ears; the heart does not love, nor does the mind love through the heart. This heart was so raw, so damaged, all love was destroyed in her mind, yet still, and so puzzlingly to her, she still had so much love. Obvious to me then, that love, real love, Unconditional Love, her love had to be coming from her Soul. Was there anywhere else it could possibly stem from? Not heart, not her troubled mind, not liver, lungs or even big toe; I was convinced her Soul was the source. So I thanked mine for making sense of those two 'confronting' clients, and for the way that I was being guided slowly, but oh so surely toward a totally new understanding of the capacity of my total being.

Why has my tapping stopped here? All I am drawn to is the word total, surely that is simple enough, who needs that defined for them? But there is no key to press now and so, TOTAL *complete, comprising the whole.* Once again, thank you, that is it. I was being gently pushed along the road to completeness; slowly coming to the conscious (CONSCIOUS *aware, knowing*) belief that I could find wholeness; which acknowledgement, as a matter of course, had to go hand in hand with the one that acknowledged a previous incompleteness. I always knew something was missing and I've told you how I spent a large proportion of my life believing that sometime, somewhere I was going to find a someone so wise who would sort everything for me, who would unravel all the mysteries and answer all those unanswerable questions; would in fact complete me. What a fool I felt when at last I realised that the person I had been so tirelessly seeking outside, somewhere else in the world, anywhere in fact but under my very own nose, was right here. Right with me, part of me, within me, my own personal possession here inside me, my Soul, the missing part, the last piece in my jigsaw, my puzzle; the part that could complete the whole and would complete the whole. The whole, therefor wholesome self, the total, complete being that is me, in fact just exactly what I had set out in search of all those years ago. What an amazing circular journey, you could have knocked me down with a feather (again) when I realised that I WAS BACK WITH MYSELF.

Goodness knows when I left me. If we have many incarnations, as I feel we do, then it could have been thousands of years ago. If we only exist here the once then I surmise that I most likely 'went off' in babyhood; whatever the timing it doesn't seem that important to me. I was beginning to believe that within myself lay the possibility of finding the 'wise one' I had sought and that that was the best place to be. Every day my Soul, when I listened properly, was putting answers into my conscious mind for me to hear; every day new things came to light and each time that happened I soared with joy. I thought I now knew exactly what that mysterious sought after state of enlightenment truly was, and it was nothing to do with meditating yourself out of your mind. It was far easier than that.

I simply believed and then acknowledged that I had a hitherto unrecognised element to my being, in practical terms another 'organ' in my body. Each time I had any physical or mental sensation (feeling) that took over my attention I gave it to my Soul, feeling it, and 'shining' the light of my Soul (Unconditional Love) to the affected part, and sure as 'eggs is eggs' sooner, or in a while, my conscious mind gave me the answers. You might call these flashes of inspiration, I say the light dawned, enlightenment, and with that came each time a real sense of becoming lighter, a most definite feeling of less heaviness in my body and a definite sense of upping the wattage in my mind. Those two things I believe made it possible to begin to experience joy, and then more joy, in fact occasionally I felt so joyous I thought I might take off. It was very exciting though, not dangerous (in terms of flying away I mean.)

This was only the beginning of my life with my Soul, and I had, and still have, some way to go before I can say that I live in balance of brain and Soul with harmony of mind and body. To tell you the truth there are times when I feel I have made no headway at all and wonder if perhaps I am that 'loony' from 'loony-go-round', but those times are fewer and farther between now. I know now that whatever happens I am sold on my Soul, and in testing times (for that is what I believe they are, tests of my resolve) in those times I know that temporarily my negative mind set, my out of balance ego is working overtime to reassert himself in his former position of supreme power. "No go, old chap" and I smile inwardly at him, as I'm very fond of my ego, in the right place, in tandem with my Soul. I know that I'd be no good without him, in the way that I was no good with my Soul so overshadowed. So with a growing realisation of what had been given to me the day that box of cards was handed over, I looked forward to my weekly time at the shop in the 'readers' booth.

Hardly anyone came, but, as I realised very quickly that the profound effects the cards had and the subsequent openings for healing were not best dealt with in a part public environment, I had little sadness. My ego was OK too, helped by the fact that the shop was dying, and a few weeks after I started there it was closed down. In case you are worrying, the owner took on smaller premises in a busier location and has done much better since. It did though leave me once again by the roadside, looking, though much less anxiously now, for the next bus.

Well, I couldn't have been standing in the right place, in my complacency, in my new found optimism, in my eagerness and excitement at the possibilities that had been put before me, I must have stepped out into the road, for suddenly I was hit broad-side and flattened.

Depression, that which I believed was a thing of the past, something I had most definitely left far behind slammed back with a vengeance and slayed me. Now what? What the hell was going on now? Were all my ideas, my theories, my beliefs, my truths crap? How could this possibly be happening now, again? I'd been working so hard, struggling for so long; believed finally I had got somewhere, hadn't I? I was on the road to something good, wasn't I? Not just for myself, but for any-one else who crossed my path with a weary body and mind, but with hope in their Soul.

I was learning about touching Souls, listening to Souls, linking with Souls and joining Souls with the greater Universal Soul in the glorious condition of Unconditional Love. I was learning of the power, supreme, ultimate, that this energy, free in us all and freely available around us, offers. SUPREME *greatest possible,* ULTIMATE *last, final, beyond which no other exists or is possible.* As always my dictionary speaks it clearly. Unconditional Love is the energy of the Soul, there is simply nothing, absolutely nothing greater existing, nothing greater possible. Can you imagine how excited I was capable of feeling while the trail of that was fresh ahead of me? In fact I was much more than excited when time after time my theories seemed to me to be confirmed by the events and then the insights into myself and in my life.

So, if you can begin to imagine my euphoric state of eager anticipation of what each new day might bring then you may also be open to the horror and shocked disbelief that this black mantle had crept up from behind and engulfed me again. You may have a guess at the fun my negative ego had at that time, so much in fact that I forgot all about the discovery of my Soul. Just for a while. It was only a little while, because, as I now know, once you have acknowledged its existence, its power, its love, there is absolutely no way that you forget or don't hear it, eventually. Every time you clear away some shadow the voice of your Soul is heard louder and the light of its love shines brighter. There is really no escaping it; who in their right mind would want to?

That is really a clue to the whole thing. We live, mostly not in our 'right mind' but in the negative mind of our conditioning and that is always, yes (I am definite about this statement) yes, always based on fear. Human beings live beneath the umbrella energy of fear, to a lesser or larger degree. If we have experienced anyone living totally in fear, acting that out, we often describe them as 'heartless beasts'. I guess we view them as not totally human, most definitely without love. What we are experiencing is a person who is temporarily out of touch with their Soul, a person who functions totally within the energy of fear,

Soul Listening

with no access to the energy of Unconditional Love. This is a very frightening experience for both the person in the grip of total fear and anyone in their orbit; it is always destructive and sometimes lethal.

So it was in my own world of fear, jibed at by my overbearing ego, until suddenly I heard that sweet voice. "Remember what you think you are learning Beth, use what you know has worked before, gather the power of your mind to tune into this shadow from the depths, feel it with all the processes of your brain, know it as your own feeling, acknowledge it as yours, as part of you, nothing to fear, nothing to disown, just something to know." So I used my brain to 'look' at the symptoms of my depression, to analyse the feelings of it, to think about the physical feelings that this depression was causing in my body. I was busy involved in the concentrated efforts that were required to analyse the sensations that were going on in my body, busy using my brain to look at and feel something that has been described as a mental illness, very busy with my brain fully absorbed in its tasks of analysis. Further brain busy with the concentrated visual effort of using the Unconditional Love light of my Soul to shine on each injured part of my being, while silently speaking the words that were acknowledging that the symptoms of depression that I was experiencing were shadows from the past, although none the less real then. I was reliving feelings from childhood (and before) knowing they belonged to the past, feeling my reactions to events, learning about and accepting my conditioning. I did not have to go on living with the past; my Soul could 'shine' away that shadow.

Suddenly, in the midst of all that mental effort I was aware that I had no symptom. SYMPTOM *perceptible change in the body or its function, indicating injury or disease; sign or token of the existence of something.* No dis-ease. DIS *apart, away, not, absence of state,* EASE *freedom from pain or trouble.* Just like that, in a minute or so I was at ease, and bursting with the birth of a new seed of inspiration, a new theory was taking place in my mind for what I realised was that my depression was not a brain condition. How could it be? I had been using all the faculties of my brain in a sparklingly clear, lucid, controlled way and anyone who has experienced depression knows that these are the qualities which are first to go. One is not sparkling, not clear and definitely not reasoning. So, how if I was experiencing depression, a malfunction of the brain, was I able to function in such a normal way? I was mentally alert, perceptive and in my opinion as normal and sane as I am usually. It seemed to me then that 'mental illness' (disturbance/unbalance of the mind) is a symptom, the end result of something other than the brain malfunctioning. I was able to use the functions of my brain exactly as normal which suggests to me that those mind disturbances are symptoms of a different 'dis-ease'. Mind (the dictionary is no help here.)

At this point in the tappers progress things on the screen went into complete disorder, in print (now scrapped) it was an utter muddle and my attempts to turn it into coherent prose only served to, to use a modern idiom, do my head in. Yet this felt extremely important to me, I wanted you to understand it as I had. The more I puzzled, the more I tried to pull the text into shape, the more clarity evaded me; until I sat quietly with my dictionary. Here are the notes I wrote.

MENTAL ILLNESS *disorder of the mind*
DISORDER *confused*

MUDDLE *disorder*
DISORDER *confused*
CONFUSED *thrown into disorder*

CONFUSE *throw into disorder, make indistinct, mix up in the mind, mentally decrepit*
INDISTINCT *obscure* (out of sight - SOUL?) OBSCURED *hidden, remote from observation; unnoticed*
DECREPIT *wasted, worn out*
WASTED *act of wasting, ineffective use* (of SOUL?)

Clear sight ensued: but back to the text.

Symptoms all have a cause. Where or what was the cause? Why and how had I known mental dis-ease? What was I apart from? What was the state absent in me? Where was the pain and trouble stored? If I could answer all these questions, would it be found that some-one as seriously pained as my psychotic father had the same reason for his 'dis-ease' as I had? Was 'mental illness' after all like the piece of string I had long since suspected it to be? A piece of string, called negative conditioning on which we all stand, somewhere along its length. The most balanced at one end, the psychotic at the other end. Could I better understand what might be going on if I now called my piece of string FEAR? Is mankind living slightly in fear, moderately in fear or totally in fear? This seemed a likely answer.

From my knowledge and experience of the psychotic (most seriously 'mentally ill') I was convinced that at the lowest episodes, the worst suffering, the times of experiencing hell were those when the sufferer was immersed in all encompassing fear. Yet even in those worst scenarios, this was not a completely constant state; there was occasionally some release from the grip of fear. Something else, something that had power over fear, something exerted its strength from time to time to save the person in question.

I spent days bombarding myself with questions. The idea that the Soul was at the bottom of all this had been immediate, but sorting out the details took a lot longer. In my belief the Soul energy was Unconditional Love and I was confronted here with the energy of fear. If as I suspected, the source of those mental symptoms was the Soul, that conflicted with the Soul being the source of Unconditional Love. I concentrated my thoughts again on that strange experience of monitoring my symptoms of depression: a depressed state of mind or a depressed mind? DEPRESS *push or pull down, lower.* What gets pushed or pulled down? As my Dad might have said, depress on. Pushed or pulled down on; on what?

I tried to work out how I had looked at my depression with a mind that was not experiencing that depression. I was feeling it; that was it. So began the analysis of feelings, a word we all use frequently to describe things that are quite intangible. INTANGIBLE *cannot be touched, cannot be grasped mentally.* Yet feelings, (FEELING *physical sensation*) feelings are, in the pure sense of the word, very real, they are physical. Depression had manifested itself in me as real physical symptoms, feelings; the descent into it, the overpowering from behind I felt in my body in a real, physical way.

Looked at in this light feelings seemed synonymous with physical symptoms which are produced by the brain. It seemed to me that we could easily muddle feelings with emotions, the real with the intangible. If I am pricked on the arm I may feel hurt. What I really feel is the bodily response, via my brain, of the pain caused by a needle rupturing the skin membrane. By saying I feel hurt, I am expressing an emotion, not a feeling. Our brain via the chemical and neurological reactions senses physical feelings but something else responds with emotion. We say we feel sick with love, we feel raw with the cold, numb with shock etc., etc., physical feelings triggered in the brain, emotional responses triggered elsewhere. Just as the emotion of love cannot be coming from the organ of the heart, I believe that the emotions attached to other things cannot be coming from that computer of a brain.

People will probably be agreeing, even shouting "well of course not, silly woman, we all know these things come from the mind." OK but what is the mind? Does anyone know? Is it any more than a concept? Has any-one seen a mind? No of course not, any more than any-one has seen a Soul; but although we have all experienced the mind, creations of the mind, power of the mind, I defy any-one to prove to me what a mind is. As I said, even my trusty dictionary companion struggles with this word. That is why I feel no need to make any attempt to try to prove to you the existence of the Soul. You all know I have no chance. I can only tell you of my experience of the Soul, of its creations, its power and of my belief in its energy of Unconditional Love.

I have proved it to myself. My proof finally came that day when, I believe, every useable inch of my brain was fully employed feeling the physical, brain induced sensations in my body and 'looking' at my depression: every construct of my mind was working over-time, when something from somewhere blew that dreadful black cloud clean away.

I have not been doing my tapping for a day or two, but I have been learning. Well I hope I have been. Perhaps it is more correct to say that what has transpired in my life during the last five days was another chance to learn some of the lessons of my life, not general knowledge but things specific to my personal highway. I would love to be able to say that I have learnt the lessons offered to me, but I know from past experience that I am slow to learn. I know that in the past I have found myself on what I have felt and described as my treadmill. Round and round it went and I was always so disappointed when familiar landscapes passed by me as I floundered round, round and then round again; small wonder that I spent an enormous chunk of my life feeling physically sick and permanently in a state of digestive disorder. I was literally unable to swallow, to digest the things that were being fed to me, but despite constant misery and dis-ease I still did not learn the lessons.

It is very different now, I have just enjoyed the opportunity that I was given to have another go. Yes that really is true, I have experienced glowing joy from the pain of the lesson; oh, not while it was happening. In the past the circumstances would have been at the least embarrassing and at the most utterly mortifying, but now I live with my acknowledged Soul none of those emotions came into it. They belong to the negative ego, which gets weaker all the time. Conversely each time he makes up his mind to gather his forces for another desperate attack on my resources, he manages to summons extra power, like the force of a dying gasp and with that throws all hell at me. That may or may not be the true scenario; it may be that now things are so sweet his attacks are thrown into sharp contrast; they may be no worse, they may just appear so against the peace of what I now experience. Whatever the truth of that, the reality was that one minute I was sailing gleefully along with the wind of good fortune pushing gently from behind, not a hint of rocks, squalls or storms and the next minute all those things hit me in the face. They sprang as it seemed from nowhere, caught me full on and felled me.

In ordinary language, I burst into tears in front of my client and the landscape contractors; (I'm creating a beautiful garden) the first time a Soul shadow has emerged with such publicity. I could not stop the eruption of emotion, and in truth I didn't particularly want to, nor did I apologise, I felt no need for that, nor did I feel any shame. I did leave the scene as quickly as was appropriate, I wanted to get home to look at that Soul shadow.

I knew that was what it was, for I acknowledged some time ago that our emotional patterns, the reactions to our life events that we bury when we don't know how to deal with them are laid down like shadows over our Souls. These negative emotions (Soul Shadows) are the things that make it difficult for the Unconditional Love of the Soul to get out; this energy of the Soul is pro-active, creative, the source of growth and thus personal fulfilment.

Soul Listening

Emotions come to mind, they are not stored there. Memories come to mind of the physical feelings attached to all emotional experiences (good as well as bad) memories produced by the mechanical processes of the brain, memories not emotions. The brain is re-active not pro-active. It reacts to our experiences by putting in action a set of physical responses, tears, lump in the throat, sweating, dizziness, every physical happening that you can imagine is the brain's reaction. From these pro-active and re-active sources the mind is developed.

As I had grown to believe that each event in life, in our outer world, mirrors the personal inner world, I knew the moment my tears formed that the play that had unfolded, the storm that had blown up in my face was a wonderful opportunity to know and then dissolve another of my Soul Shadows. Another hitherto hidden emotional problem could be understood and in the understanding, the knowing, could be banished from my being. My Soul had created this opportunity. I had been given two clear signals to help me avoid the disaster; my mind had heard the warning voice of my Soul on both occasions and my mind, in negative conditioned mode had over-ridden that wise, helpful voice. Twice, I had ignored it. The only way left, if I was ever going to learn, was the painful way, the normal, usual way of any human learning.

I'm coming to the conclusion that this painful human process is not the only way to learn. I can't put that forward yet as my confirmed belief as so far I keep missing the opportunity to use the easy option; to listen to my Soul (which I do) to hear it (which I do) and to act on that (which I don't, yet.)

When my emotions so openly erupted I knew they were not coming from my mind, for my mind was 'watching' the scene, analysing it, noticing that I was not experiencing any of the 'pain' of my usual symptoms of dented ego, wounded pride etc.. My mind was simply experiencing for me the players in their parts acting out this Soul Shadow. So back home I let my mind, my brain and my body experience the emotion of the Shadow in whatever form it took, and it would not have been a pretty sight for any onlooker. It would most certainly have worried some, but these things are private between my mortal being and my immortal being. The result was that an hour later found me having a cuppa and a few minutes rest, feeling much lighter, and much much brighter, though as yet no more enlightened in my mind as to what all the fuss had been about. But I now have so much more experience of the power of my Soul and knew that in its own time, as long as I kept listening, my mind would hear and know the content of that Shadow. Sure enough, it came bit by bit over the course of the next day. I always write down what comes to mind, it is my way of acknowledgement of the truth, and I always write thank you.

I saw that I had learnt two or three lessons at that one time; they were all connected as they always are. It's like finding pieces of a jig-saw puzzle and each time being able to fit them immediately in the right place, and watching as the picture gets nearer completion and becomes so much clearer. I don't know if the complete picture is a possibility, I do hope so, it's so exciting. What I do know is that as my incomplete image gets the pieces filled in, my own power grows and my ability to harness the wonder of Unconditional Love, Soul energy, grows and grows. This really does rub off in those around me, I can see it, and I can feel it. Good energy is being generated, created.

Tapping out the word created is bringing me gently back to where I was the other day, talking about depression and mental illness. I was stuck with it, no tapping was forth-coming; so I sent a message on the screen to ask for help. I didn't know what was going on then, but now looking back I see that I wrote "can you please help me tomorrow, am I meant to be doing this alone"? As I said I had come to a grinding halt with the tapping and so decided to leave the machine for that day, (probably before my 'promised hour') after asking for help the next day. I meant help on the machine with the tapping!

The next day help was at hand. That was the day the storm broke while I was creating a garden and yes, in one sense I certainly did have to 'be doing this alone'. I alone had something to experience before I could continue the tapping. In the true sense I was far from alone, I had my Soul by my side and it was lovely spending those four days in the right company. As well as being lovely I was able to experience, again, what I am coming to understand as the source of what we know as 'mental illness'.

CREATE *bring into existence* CREATIVE *able to create*, that is, able to bring into existence. I say the Soul is able to bring into existence. EXISTENCE *being, yes* BEING. The thing we were urged to be doing all those years ago in the groups where spiritual growth was so ardently sought. Being, just being. I really did not have the vaguest idea what that meant then, and because of that ignorance I was unable to have a go at being. I don't know if others had the same difficulties as I did, I suspect they did; but no-one speaks out, do they? No-one wants to be seen as not understanding, no one wants to show their fear. I was always asking questions, joking about my short comings, my inability to quite see exactly what was meant by all the new concepts and ideas. There was so much I did not understand.

Here I am again, returning to my opening dialogue about my own lack of understanding of so many things; this leads me to thoughts about communication. Communicating through language is, or has generally been believed to be the way in which human beings make contact to express anything and everything to their fellows; that said, it should I believe follow that in order for communication (by spoken or written word) to be at all effective the words offered should be understood by the recipient in the way that the deliverer intends. I don't believe this happens nearly as often as it should or could.

Read here a long gap; despite my resolve and every good intention it has been some weeks since I have completed my daily tapping. The break has made me think, mostly about what could be 'going on'. The last time this happened to me I enjoyed a chance to learn (or perhaps more accurately I should say, a chance to practise again) one of my life's lessons. I have since then repeated the mistake, that is to say, not acted on the knowledge I was convinced that I now understood and in the understanding would never repeat again. But I am human and I err. On one level, on a deeper level, I guess that Soul Shadows that are really dense take quite a bit of shifting; some of mine lie like lead caskets.

I hoped the break from this which truly feels enforced, (I have actually opened up my file and found my stopping place on this great toilet roll of words and then someone has called, the phone has rung and one way or another I have been physically taken from my chair) would have been a gap for enlightenment to fill. I hoped something would happen that would strengthen my Soul purpose, build my ability to fly back to these keys with renewed fervour, startling new findings and the ability to portray with spellbinding clarity my theory of mental disorder. But no, nothing, and I find apprehension has taken hold of me, my contact with the Soul that guides these tapped words is tenuous.

I don't like the feelings, they are feelings of fear. I fear I will not succeed in this venture, on my own I am useless, my mind is clouded, not exactly empty for it hurts in my head with a dull confused heaviness, which starts to become panic as I search for coherent thoughts and the words of those thoughts. I try to make my Soul contact. That does not work as usual. Has my negative mind found some extra power? What has really kept me from the joyous tapping of the past months when I happily tried to keep up with the flow of words given to me to tap out? Have I lost my trust? Have my beliefs wavered? Has my ego regained the power in what I thought was a more balanced new relationship, the harmonious coupling of body and Soul? Was that all delusion?

Agreed it was only my idea, only my theory, only tried and tested by myself and a few people who have come to me. If this theory and the subsequent limited study were put to the test it would be ridiculed as a severely flawed study indeed. Perhaps I have been deluded? My vision, the clarity with which I (thought) was seeing and understanding things is now so clouded, I feel it slipping out of my grasp. I feel that I am completely unable to bring the two things, that is, the power of my intellect, my reasoning, and my conditionally fearful mind on the one hand and the soaring, visionary, power of the creative Soul on the other, together. I can only sense the uselessness of my mind, without the positive balance of harmony with my Soul, and feel the strength of my conditioned mind's ability to take control of me in a frightening way.

If I didn't know better, at this very moment I would be telling you that I feel that I am losing my mind. Let me try to describe that to you (those of you who experience mental problems will be all too familiar with the effects of such disturbance.) I feel almost as though I am in another world, a world of unreality, unreal because I have no control over this other world, the world I am experiencing in my here and now mind. My head, mostly the brain area of my head, is home to physical feelings that have overpowered any ability that I usually have to think in any way that resembles normal, rational thought. I can quite literally feel part of my mind trying to fight its way through the fog of sensations that have filled it; I am almost out of my mind for I am able to sense some part of me trying to get back into it. It is quite, quite horrible and I know that under different circumstances (those being, if I had not consciously acknowledged the existence of my Soul and the power and protection of Unconditional Love that it gives to me, and believed that) I would be doing something very bizarre to get away from these overwhelmingly tormenting feelings. Now, in this state I understand what I have witnessed in my fellow man ripping clothes off with a knife, damaging, to the point of total destruction and even trying to dispense with other human beings. The disturbance I am watching and understanding in my head is overpowering, who wouldn't try anything to escape that?

I find I have stopped to rub my poor head many times while tapping these few lines and each time I do so a vision of my father and other memories of sorely troubled 'souls' doing exactly the same thing, is before me. I stop again to rub my head really hard, it makes no difference to the feelings, and I try to imagine how this particular type of torment would affect anyone, on a long term basis. I glance at the clock and am amazed to find that an hour has passed, I have lost all sense of time, all sense of outside reality, I experience only the confusion in my head; it is truly terrible.

I thank my Soul that I can return to normality, just like that, and I do.

And I now know why I was kept from my tapping for so long. I was busily occupied creating a very large garden, putting harmony and beauty where previously there was only potential. I was effecting transformation, working with nature and giving my knowledge and help with love. The joy in me verged on Unconditional Love, perfect conditions for growth in every sense of the word, and as the outer mirrors the inner, this was the perfect place for growth and transformation in me. It was also, as it had to be, the one place where I was confident that my knowledge, my expertise and my ability would be 'heard' and 'listened' to; they weren't! To my clients, my family and any other onlookers of that personal growth period it must have appeared that my 'apple cart' had been well and truly overturned. For a little (tiny, little while) it felt like that to me also, until I learned the most profound lesson so far and found many, many more of those missing pieces of my puzzle. Without the balance in my being that that enlightenment afforded I could not have stepped safely into today's realms of mental disturbance.

At this moment I am not sure of the significance of the experience which I have tapped my way through, though as with my 'exploits' into fear, to experience is to know; so I trust in the value of this interlude and offer it for both of us.

Today is yesterday's tomorrow, which has become now; and before I can write, now, that has gone, it is the past, almost as though there is no now at all, ever. I am in contemplative mood, I very often am. I have been pondering the experience at this screen yesterday. There are a few words that occupy my cranium which I realise have been in residence for a few weeks, the same few simple little words that have been on the merry-go-round of my mind since I began, what feels like, that enforced break in tapping out this tale of mine. BREAK *make or become discontinuous (otherwise than by cutting or tearing) divide or disperse into two (or more) parts.* What a seemingly simple little word, it has haunted me for weeks, taken weeks to listen to, really listen that is, yet there it is in front of me reminding me that I had become discontinuous. CONTINUOUS *connected, unbroken; uninterrupted in time or sequence,* all these things I have not been in terms of my purpose to tap an hour a day. I have been discontinuous and more importantly I have felt discontinuous; during which time the ego, that master of the negative conditioning, jumps in. "What are you doing Beth? do you really know what you are doing? who are you anyway? are you qualified? where are your degrees? your experience? who is going to be in the slightest bit interested in what you, a nonentity, think about? who will want to read about your life? and who will take your isolated theories seriously? anyway, haven't you noticed, Soul is everywhere, you're too late Beth, you were given this two years ago, what the hell have you been up to since then? The band wagon has left and you weren't on it, you don't have anything new to add now" and so on, so relentlessly on.

Was the break I have endured enforced, as it felt? could I have avoided it? can I answer that? To answer the latter first, no, I could not have avoided it, nor do I wish that I had, it was another chance to learn and become lighter, a chance to look at some Soul Shadows of mine, again. Doubtless I will be looking again and again and again, until they become so thin, so transparent that I will not notice them at all. You may be questioning this, you may wonder if I really am having any positive effect on the debilitating Soul Shadows. I am. I can honestly say that each time I experience the result of some former negative conditioning I encounter it in a much more positive way.

In the past, the things that have occurred recently could well have caused me to give up my venture. Don't get me wrong, by nature I am not a quitter, the menial, physical and psychological tasks I have faced and stuck with bear witness to that; rather than sinking into the mire of despondent failure I have always thrown myself headlong into some enormous physical challenge which a man twice my size would be proud of.

Now, neither of those things happen, I go quietly, happily and peacefully about my business, and my 'business' seems so much more rewarding than ever it did before. I don't chastise myself, and though I hear the harsh words that my ego feeds me, they really don't have any lasting effect on me at all. I need my ego, it drives the essence of me that is human, but I definitely do not need that negatively conditioned, oversized, self-important, fearful aspect of it; and it knows that. It will doubtless not be accepting the new situation and its new role; it has been in charge of me for too long and enjoyed its power over me, so I am expecting trouble. But though I know the possibilities, though I know what gruesome constructs it can create, I have no fear; not since I experienced the power of Unconditional Love and tasted the positive creativity of that energy.

I come back to that little word, break, and to the journey that took me on. BREAK *divide,* DIVIDE *separate into, or in parts, split or break up,* BREAK *disperse,* DISPERSE *scatter, go or send in different directions.* Here, still in that same five letter word is more and more information about the situation, the scene if you like, that was playing before me and playing for me if I cared to take notice.

The life that we see around us each and every day really does act as a window to our inner world, if only the glass were kept a little cleaner, if only we looked more often, if only we understood the value of looking, if only we truly believed the statement. I have been so busy listening for the past two years, that I've only recently become consciously aware of the lessons (the enlightenment) on offer when I look. I'm beginning to wonder, with excitement and anticipation, what will come next?

Break; the thing I knew I was experiencing, and was a bit uncomfortable with, as I really did not want to experience it. That break was given to be understood at as many levels as I was prepared to 'see' it, with every meaning that the dictionary can supply: so many aspects to something so small. I was divided, in that I was enjoying my new found position as creator and in doing so I did not manage to create the space in my days for this 'creation'. I was

Soul Listening

dispersed, off in different directions as people, who offered opportunities for me to achieve some practical improvements in my home, unexpectedly presented themselves. I was definitely discontinuous, at a time when what I really wanted above all was to continue with my theory on the cause, the nature and following naturally from that, the cure for mental illness. Continuation was not forthcoming, and as I come round again to the point of continuation I feel the separation from my flow.

I recall telling you how when I read some of the words that I had tapped they were so disappointing to me; they had no lustre, they conveyed none of the qualities that my thoughts, my ideas, my personal revelations had when they were images in my mind. That was a blow, but perhaps a lesson also. It made me think about the qualities of music, painting, etc., and I wondered whether any of us ever experience a creation in the way that the creator does? I do know that different things 'speak' to different people, though in contradiction, when something is truly of great beauty it moves the majority. I couldn't see my words moving anyone or conjuring anything in the imagination, comparing them to the images of my mind they seemed dead. Yet I have only words to give to you; or do I?

Can I write with Unconditional Love? I know the times when my conditioned ego gets in the way, I feel the times when my Soul is in charge of this. Maybe you sense those times? Perhaps the problem stems from my concept of the theory I have been working on for these two years; I have been thinking of it as mine. I have believed myself to have conceived the notion; understandable I think as I have been the one to go through the experiences that have enabled a theory to be born, but the truth is that the idea only came into being when Soul made its contact with me. I have no doubt that the universal Soul was responsible for this, at least that would explain to me how I was at last able to hear the voice of my own Soul which alone had not yet managed to penetrate my thick skull.

The theory (simplicity itself) was born out of Soul contact; yes, the bodily experiences were mine, the mental traumas were mine, the experiencing and gaining knowledge of the human driving energy of conditioned negativity - FEAR- were mine; but the thing that kept me going through all that, kept me going, surviving and growing stronger, took me to the place where I could sit in complete trust and tap out these words, with no preparation or thought, was, and is, my Soul. My Soul was the vehicle that I waited for at the bus stops of my life, and my Soul's pathway is the route I travel. When I succeed in finding the balance of brain and Soul in my mind we will fly where now I dither. I guess I had to dither in this also, to have those breaks and difficulties with the tappers flow, until I become undivided, until I find total harmony and balance of my two parts, until I acknowledged true ownership of the theory that felt so important to me, and my ego.

I am happy to work with that, but I hope it doesn't take too long to get back in shape. Not because I may miss some boat of self-promotion, but because I can't wait to see what will happen next.

I have been at the optician's today, keeping an eye on the young son's sight. Having missed the signs of my daughter's short-sightedness and only really become aware of her problems long after they should have been dealt with, (by a more vigilant parent) I am now almost over zealous in my protection, running for check ups at the first sight of headaches and squints. All is fine and as it should be. I think back and wonder how I could have missed all the obvious signs and signals that my daughter gave out. I look back with feelings of guilt, after all was it not my duty to care and protect? How could it come about that someone as caring and protective as I know myself to be missed the message that was before my eyes in her eyes?

There were mitigating circumstances (there always are, aren't there?) We had been living out of suitcases for two years, living with extra worries and problems; I was occupied more with day to day survival than providing for our long-term future. In this climate my mind was overly full, clouded, confused; my life was so extra-ordinary, so out of the ordinary that my mind, responding in kind, was obviously not focused on the ordinary, the usual or the norm. There definitely was no norm to those two years; I felt as though I had died and arrived in hell, but it was just a living hell, which as the years passed was almost becoming a new norm for me.

My daughter meanwhile did not mention the difficulties she must have been having trying to see the blackboard from the back of the room. Now I wonder why? Another instance of having so little regard for self, suffering in silence rather than rocking the boat, even gently? Or was it through ignorance? If you do not see clearly and that is all you have ever known, then would you come up with the idea that the way that you are seeing things is not the correct way? Do we ever question the things that are outside our scope of experiences? Did I stop to question myself, to ask myself whether her sight was as it should be? No, of course not, why should I? There was no reason to; no precedent of short-sightedness to my knowledge in the family.

Do we stop to question anything at all; all the time things appear to be functioning in a normal manner? I think not, unless and until we have had the experience of something that does not conform to the normal, acceptable, understood to be correct pattern. Then, we are alerted, you could say awakened, to the possibilities. Just like me today, double-checking the eye-sight in order to avoid any problem that could be hijacked by prompt action, doubtless in order to avoid my making the same mistake twice. My previous experience had enlightened me.

What do you think of my using such an apparently significant 'spiritual' word to describe something as mundane as that small human lesson that I am telling you about? I'll tell you what I think; I think that knowledge is enlightenment. No, I don't mean the knowledge of books and learning; in some ways those things can be elitist, they are not open to every-one for a number of reasons. That cannot be the way to enlightenment as that precludes too many of us, and surely there are no barriers to enlightenment, no distinctions, no rules to state who can and who cannot achieve this state of being-ness.

That experience, though a simple one, gave me knowledge, through which I gained power, the power to make a decision, draw a conclusion and act on that, and the action I took was a direct result of the enlightenment of the experience, enlightenment in the truest sense of the word. ENLIGHTEN *instruct, inform, shed light on, give light to, free (person) from prejudice or superstition, hence enlightenment.* As the book says, this person was freed from prejudice. Freed of the ignorance that was mine through lack of knowledge; having no previous experience of any sight problems, thus owning a preconceived opinion (superstition) that eyes were perfect and operated perfectly without any special attention or care.

So today, here with you, I have added another belief to my truth; enlightenment comes from the knowledge gained through personal experience. No human experience is too unimportant that it can be denied a part in my book of knowledge.

I could not imagine why today I sat to tell you about my trip to the optician. It seemed to me a most mundane thing to recount, but as always the wise Soul that guides me over these keys has taught me some things that I was not consciously aware of until now. Now I begin to understand those words that so bugged me before, the words 'just be'. They seemed so patronising when offered to me before, without new experience, without new knowledge. I really wanted to scream out "what do you mean, 'just be'; tell me how I can 'just be'?" There were no answers, just as in my therapy; there are no answers to be given by others only answers to be personally found. My ego wonders whether sharing these discoveries as I make them is any more use to you than the 'just be's' 'go with the flow's' and 'love yourself's' that were handed to me; they were utterly useless at the time, though doubtless given with good intentions!

This morning I lost it. What exactly do I mean by that? I've been pondering that question from then until now. Well perhaps not that precise question, not, what do I mean by those words but what does the fact that I lost it mean to me? What is the significance of my losing it and more importantly just what is it that I lost? Part of that is easy to answer, you probably know the answer, for don't we all now and then 'lose it'? Would we be human if we didn't? Only an angel could get through the sometime mire of human existence and remain calm, loving, gracious, understanding and forgiving, couldn't it? Only an angel or some-one so in tune and in touch with what some call the 'higher' side of human nature, (the Unconditional Love of the Soul) that come what may, come what mire, they never loose touch, never loose sight, never loose contact with those wonderful qualities.

Therein lay my answer. Before me I see the reason for this morning's experience of 'losing it', and here I was thinking to take you through the hours of my day as I've pondered the many layers of significance to the event which lasted only a few minutes. It was no more than that, a few minutes of one day, not much in a week, less proportion of a month, decreasing in size through a year, smaller than ever in a decade and soon totally lost in the span of a life-time; just a spec of experience, less than a blink of time but holding a lesson of such importance that I am in awe. You see, I could have missed it so easily. I know that I've missed similar opportunities countless, innumerable times before, yet this one I saw. No, that's not true, heard? No, that's not right either. I felt it. That is how it gained my attention; I felt it, so deeply and so strongly that the impact of the feeling has not left me for hours. I have been feeling the 'losing it' and thinking on its significance.

So, what was it that caused me to lose it? In the analysis of the events I see I was under pressure, having problems with the youngest son. I often remind myself that there has been very little time since he became known to my womb that he has not caused me worry, anxiety, feelings of pain, and occasionally, like this morning, the thought that I wished for nothing more than to be left in peace, to be free from the problems that he has.

How to intellectualise the 'losing it'. Did I lose patience? Yes. Did I lose the ability to control myself? Yes, Did I lose rationality and reason? Yes; yes, to all those things and any that you can think of. Why did I lose those conditions of adulthood and the tools of responsible parenting? I definitely didn't stop loving, though I know that briefly I wanted to. That would have made it easier for me, to stop loving, to stop caring, to stop having the responsibility of a child with needs that I could not meet, (at that moment I probably felt as though I had never been able to meet his great needs.) I see that I lost those things because I had them. Well, it is impossible to lose something that you have never had. I also lost touch with all the skills that I really needed to help him through a troubling patch, because I felt a complete failure, I simply did not know how to make things right for him. I felt inadequate and useless, entrusted with the welfare of this precious child and once more, as I have been so very many times in his life, unable to put things right for him. So I flipped, ranting my inadequacy, raging my frustrations and losing control. I threw a slipper at him; a very soft one.

It's not always immediate, the realisation of lessons, not yet. I'd rather call them opportunities, chances to be more angelic next time; pushes in the direction of the Soul, ways to show me what I need to see. As soon as I looked I saw that fear was getting me in its grip again, the only possible explanation for losing it with my dear son, my fear for him. My fear about the part I play in his fears (or the part I perceive myself not to be playing adequately, hence the mis-directed castigation.)

And why should fear be taking such a strong hold of me? Haven't I been trying to convince you that, with acknowledgement of your Soul, you have at your disposal the truly amazing healing power of your own share of the ginormous, never-ending supply of Unconditional Love? Haven't I been trying to share the way that I am learning to use this energy, for our mutual benefit? Doesn't look as though I know what I'm talking about does it? Unless I tell you more of the story that led up to today's little set to with the negative processes of the conditioned mind.

I told you that I made a pledge to sit at these keys for an hour a day until the story I feel I have to tell has been told. Once again, I've not been doing that. It all started on the slippery downhill slopes with school holidays. Do you see the significant connection? Both these events involve the smaller son. Oh, I started off with good intentions, very good, but the conditioning I often mention started its little games. Was I being a good mother sitting at my keys while he had to amuse himself? Was it his fault he was a late and in that almost an only child? Shouldn't I give him more of my time, rather than pursue my own selfish needs? He would be grown up all too quickly, plenty of time for myself then, in any case couldn't I make up my lost hours when he was back at school? And so on, and so on. I managed to ignore the thoughts for a day or two then gave in. "I must get my priorities right, I can easily make up the time".

That was not so, in fact the longer I left it the harder it was to find even that one hour a day. Not much, you might think, but the pressures of a shortfall in income and other family needs made it so easy to excuse myself, and in consequence it became harder and harder to find the time; in fact it became impossible (for that read, I could not make it possible.) The truth is that I have not sat here for, oh golly, nearly seven weeks, though I am no less busy today than I have been during that time. I'm here now because I saw only too clearly the lesson of 'losing it'.

Why did I use that phrase to describe what happened this morning? What does it really mean? What is the 'it' I had lost? What is it? Pondering the great question of the meaning of 'it' my dictionary for once was no help, so I realised that this 'it' was a very, very personal one indeed. I knew as soon as I gave 'it' thought that what I had lost was my acknowledgement of my Soul, and therefore my strong Soul connection. That was definitely it. I had become almost disconnected. Strange really, for during those seven weeks my mind had not lost sight of my Soul. I had used it many times. I thought that I was keeping the contact alive, but now I know that I wasn't really. It was a half-hearted connection and I had been filled with doubt about the validity of my beliefs, about all the things I had previously experienced that had caused me to develop those beliefs in the first place. Quite simply, I temporarily lost my trust, and the contact got weaker because of this.

But, and this bears repetition, the Soul is a wonderful thing, persistent despite my neglect, forever tapping me on the shoulder and eventually banging me on the head until I come back to my senses. Now I recall how many, many times in those last few weeks I have been tapped and banged. How many uncomfortable and worrying events I have struggled through and how each negative experience that I have accepted and learned nothing from, has in fact only served to weaken the link that I have worked so long to forge. I was 'losing heart' as we say. Actually I was losing Soul, as we all are when we feel that we are 'losing it'. Depressing? Yes, misery (real depression has completely gone now) overtook me, but I had made my Soul contact and even though it appeared that although I was willing to give that up, my Soul was not. THANK GOODNESS.

So here I am, back on the road again, taking strength from today's disaster that has turned out to be a miracle in disguise. My thanks are for the Soul wisdom that enabled me to see through that disguise, and the Soul love that never lets go of me.

I have to climb the stairs to get to this place. Perhaps it is inevitable that after so long away from my 'mission' my thoughts as I do so, climb the stairs that is, turn to questions once again. What am I writing about? More explicitly, where the heck do I go from here? Do you see how constantly the conditioned, negative ego tries to take over, to maintain its pole position of command and control? It still does with me, although I tell you that I am always working to keep a balanced mind. It's true, I constantly work at it and chivvy myself along in times of doubt because I know that a part of me that has been neglected, unused, unheard and unknown for so long is going to take more than a trite acknowledgement every now and then to become a fully integrated part of my being. Here and now in my human form I am trying to locate, to know, to understand, to use, to accept, to integrate my spiritual form; to find a way to balance in harmony my brain and my Soul, the driving engines of my human being and my spiritual being, the energy power-houses of my mortal and my immortal selves. No wonder I loose sight of this goal at times, no wonder my resolve dissolves.

I have just stopped tapping to look at the words in front of me and I am in awe of that task, though I know it is possible. I feel it in my water (as they say.) I believe this to be my way forward and I also believe that the way forward for mankind is to find our Souls. That's not quite what I mean, for of course they were never lost: forgotten, mislaid, overlooked, certainly under-used, but never, never lost.

Thinking of the under-used Soul brings to mind again the under-used intuition (sixth sense.) Isn't it common knowledge that some have a sixth sense? Why some? Why not, nearly everyone? Only a few people are denied access to their full complement of five senses, ergo, only a few may be denied access to the sixth sense. But what exactly is the sixth sense? Even in accepting its existence, we are ignorant of its purpose, its quality. How to describe this sense; that we often identify, but don't exactly define? Why not? We have well defined the others, and are all too familiar with them. We know exactly what to expect of them, and in this knowing and acceptance we use them all the time without a thought or a backward glance.

The sixth sense, that's a bit more difficult. We believe it exists, we probably think a lot of people have it and use it on more occasions than they might care to admit to; yet it is a mystery, something shrouded in in-definition. Just like my Soul (and yours) another thing without definition, no physical records, no sightings, touchings, smellings, tastings, feelings, only sensing: sensing that these things that are materially unreal, invisible in fact, are in their own way as real as anything which we acknowledge as having existence. SIXTH SENSE *(supposed faculty giving) intuitive or extra-sensory knowledge.* SUPPOSE *take for granted, assume in default of knowledge.* EXTRA-SENSORY *derived by means other than the known senses.* I am struck while defining the sixth sense by the amount that we take on trust! Intuition; in my father's way, inner tuition, to me that means teaching from within. Within where? Within what? I don't think this within teacher is my brain, or yours; I do not think we have a 'better' place lurking in the brain, some idealistic super-consciousness. It makes no sense to me, there's no logic to that; most important, no-one has proved the existence of these things. We only have our ideas on the subject. I have mine, they are my belief, which I trust in and will do until some-one offers concrete proof to the contrary. I believe our sixth sense, our faculty for extra knowledge is our Soul.

So to find the Soul. The only thing in my mind to tap is LOST SOUL. I look at those two words for a while, for having tapped 'to find the soul' and to see the only letters that came forth were 'lost soul' seems completely contrasting. Yet they insist again, lost soul. How many times have I, and you no doubt, passed, glimpsed, experienced a person who has drawn the comment "oh, poor lost soul." We express it with such deep emotion, for a being who can wring that sentiment stirs the very essence of our being, taps into our sincerest compassion.

Why? Why is it that a person with an aura of indescribable pain and suffering is described as a Soul? Not a man, woman or child, not a human being, but a Soul, and a lost Soul at that. Conversely, don't we also often on seeing a person enveloped in joy and innocence, comment along the lines "dear souls", and see children as "blessed little souls." I am not alone in this am I? So, what is happening? What do we see? What do we know? What is it that we seem to be unconsciously acknowledging? Very easily we recognise both the person out of touch with their Souls and the person who has that contact in place; almost inadvertently we have a deep understanding of the reality of the situation, yet we ignore that reality.

Don't we hear ourselves? Don't we listen? I didn't. For well over half a century I used the word 'soul' and completely ignored it; common usage never stopped me for one moment to think what I was saying.

*Have you noticed how much more it has been used during the last couple of years? Two inch leader head-lines, one foot high in shop windows, more daily usage in print and media, very common in the arts field, and positively burgeoning in the arena of 'alternatives' of all descriptions. I watch this with great glee. Personally it reinforces my belief that a new energy is slowly, but most definitely surrounding us. It is not intrusive, yet gently, so very gently insistent on gaining our attention; and it has, for in many guises Soul has become the new focus of attention, almost without those who use its name realising what is happening or even realising what they are doing in the name of Soul. That really doesn't matter. We use the parts of our physical being in this accepting way, never querying their true existence or function; that has never stopped them working. So it is with the Soul. The things that we know are. Thus, if we know we have a Soul, we do. The level at which we know this is totally unimportant, unless we wish it to be otherwise, that is the choice of each individual.

I'm not very good at accepting things at face value; mostly I like to know the nuts and bolts. Thus I cannot get away from the idea that we can recognise the Soul in a human being, yet apparently not be very interested in this amazing ability, this faculty for perception which, if we just stopped long enough to think about, would have us all gasping in awe at ourselves.

Those of you who have followed this train of thought through remember that I have already owned to being a very slow learner. Even having accepted that, and worked hard to alter it, I still reel with surprise when my lessons come round again on my own merry-go-round and I find I'm face to

Soul Listening

face with the spectre I have faced many times before. What a playground. What with that and the great seesaw of life one needs a good head for heights and a strong stomach, which of course all come from perfect balance. While I'm tapping I have pictures of a brightly coloured fantasy playground, and have probably stepped back to childhood fun; yet even here the purpose of this book is never far away. Balance, I am reminded.

Balance; the main purpose for searching for my Soul (even though I didn't know I was doing that) was to find the way to bring myself into balance. So I am drawn again to the 'lost soul' by the image of a person thus described. The eyes say it all, don't they? They appear dead, vacant, empty, dull, lifeless, no sparkle, no brightness nor shine. We instinctively know them to be 'lost souls'. Lost as in don't know their way? Lost soul as in person without their immortal, spiritual part? Both. Do we know, through the wisdom of our Souls and the emotion of Unconditional (Soul) Love, that what we are experiencing is a person who has LOST contact with his SOUL? A person who has lost his balance through this loss of contact? Balance of mind?

Well, I write that as a question, for I have no proof, in clinical terms, in the generally accepted terms of recognised studies or trials. I continually question my findings, my experiences and my flashes of enlightenment. I question the results of my Soul 'work'. Would the person whose Soul was spurred into action by the love from mine have experienced the miraculous recovery from the depths of their pain and misery if they had not met me and my Soul? Who knows? The truth of that is that no-one ever will, not with absolute certainty. It is a physical impossibility to split a person into two, to conduct the conclusive trials both of 'cause and effect' and 'no cause and the effect of that'. Therefor I can only put some thoughts your way while telling you my truths and trying to illustrate to you how my beliefs have come about.

*tapper's note: manuscript written a decade ago

I trust that the glimpses into my life that I have shared with you have demonstrated that something has kept me going, in exactly the same way countless millions of others are kept going through the adversities, struggles and traumas of the life we spend as human beings. Aren't you sometimes staggered by the endurance of others? We call it 'strength of character,' even heroic. HEROIC *having the qualities of a hero,* HERO *man of super human qualities, favoured by the gods; demigod.* Doesn't that amaze you? Part of us, something in this human form is recognising qualities in others that border on the 'god like'. Not only do we recognise it, we say it, (not very often of ourselves) we say aloud that there in another human being we see super-human qualities. SUPERHUMAN *beyond (normal) human capacity or power; higher than man.* It's all there in my dictionary, proof that, for at least as long as the meanings of the words that we use has been documented, we have understood and overtly acknowledged through our language, that man, human, has qualities synonymous with gods.

Where does this knowing come from? Our minds, driven as they are by the learnt fears of our lives, all the superficial fears of society, and those deeper ones, mostly of unknown origin? Many have put forward theories for the 'higher mind,' the 'super conscious', glorious states of 'mind' to aim for. MIND....... Phew! There is more than a column in 'that book' trying, and it definitely feels like trying, very hard, to define a simple four letter word.

The thought uppermost in my mind as I searched through the column for enlightenment was no wonder communication is such a difficult thing to do. Not only do we read and hear what we expect or want to read and hear, but we understand the things that we read and hear in the light of our individual experiences, which naturally differ. Even if one was a walking dictionary it would seem that the correct understanding of any given communication would be 'up for grabs'. It is just as (so as not to escape my attention when the tapping dries up) the machine has written in front of me in capitals, IN THE LIGHT OF OUR INDIVIDUAL EXPERIENCES. LIGHT *the natural agent that stimulates the sense of sight.* Well this time, back on track, the book has helped me. The 'light of our individual experiences' can simply read 'how we see things'.

How I see things now is in a completely new light; for everything that happens, that I feel, that I hear and see, can, as it were, be turned over to another side and then understood in a new way. We may never truly know what mind is, like any intangible thing it cannot be put under a microscope, dissected, categorised, re-produced. To me it is a way. Bear with me a moment ('way' takes up two columns of explanations which is unnecessarily complicated) while I find one that feels appropriate. WAY *unimpeded opportunity of advance* (please don't question the meaning of advance or we shall be here all day and I could well loose my way in this communication attempt.) I said mind is a way and I believe that, yet I know that many times my opportunity for advance has been impeded, and the obstruction hindering my advance has been, yes, my mind.

There are two things here, working together and at odds, complicating an issue that seems clear and simple to me; that is until I come to put it into the words that I hope will be received by you, my reader, with the same understanding that I have when offering them to you. Perhaps this is the problem. I so want you to share my understanding, even though I have spent some time acknowledging that understanding is a very personal thing of individual experience. All I can really do is share my experiences with you and trust in whatever understanding you receive from that.

So, to return to my unimpeded way, which is my hindered mind, an apparently blatant contradiction of terms. No wonder it felt complicated, for as I have said there are two elements, two parts here. I have quite often experienced my mind (definitely too often for the comfort and wellbeing of both it and my body) as a negative thing, capable of being an enemy rather than an ally, a foe to my body. Let me explain. There have been things I have not done which I know that I could have done and moreover they are things which I guess (I can only guess having no experience of what I refer to) would have made the quality of my life more rich, fulfilling, more satisfying and that means more enjoyable. Yet they were not overlooked through lack of opportunity or chance, they were discounted by the negative mind which said "unworthy, not capable," even "too good, too much fun for you." Then there were things rejected because they touched my areas of phobia, again things I could have enjoyed, been good at, contributed to society, taken more of a role among my fellow men. This rejecting was my mind in fear, a condition of mind which I believe we all have. Every single human being who has ever walked this earth has a fearful mind; (maybe an exception or two?) half the time we are not aware of this and during the other half we vaguely see it but have no idea what it is all about or where it comes from.

I have also experienced my mind as quite, quite different and would best describe these times as coming from somewhere inside, not from my head. (Here I would be placing a hand somewhere over the heart area of my chest, though I never thought that my heart played any part in this. Being down to earth and practical, I knew the heart to be a pumping station muscle.) This something 'inside' has kept me going, sometimes with strength, fortitude and almost that heroism we admire in others, and most surprisingly it kept offering me little glimmers of hope even in those darkest times when I was sure I had died and woken up in hell. That sounds very dramatic, now after the events, but talking to a friend recently, who sadly described herself there at present, I was reminded of the reality of such times.

There have very clearly been two quite different aspects to me, to my mind, two quite separated parts coming from different places. Defined as I have tried to they seem to be two sides at odds with each other, there has been no co-operation or collaboration, no working together for the good of my whole being. My fearful mind (and I suggest yours too) has striven to rule the roost, shutting out as often as possible the guiding voice of my Soul. The more it pushed and struggled for supremacy the more I suffered in my physical, mortal body and mind, yet my Soul carried on. Even in abject misery and overwhelming pain, it was there offering help, even when I ignored it; it worked on and unknown to me it gave me the strength, the will, the purpose to survive.

More than that, it kept me aware that there was 'something inside' me, something very special that every now and then shone through the gloom and put purpose and reason into the survival struggle.

Looking back I think that the light of the Unconditional Love of my Soul must have always been there, in my eyes, for others saw it and commented on my state of wellbeing. You can imagine how that puzzled me when I felt like death warmed up. It does though highlight for me, once again, the two parts of the one being; how separated they can be while never quite losing touch. That makes me think that they are designed to work together, ideally in balance and harmony, with equal influence.

When someone acts irrationally, even appearing 'mentally ill' we comment that they are 'off balance'. What exactly do we mean by that? What aspects, parts, conditions of a person thus described are not equal, matched? What has grown or diminished in proportion to cause the loss of equilibrium? When you think about it do you know the answer? A while ago I would have had no idea at all, yet would confidently proclaim some-one to be 'off-balance'. How could I be so sure? How could I make a confident judgement without the experience of these matters? Yet I did know, as we all do. I 'knew' something, as we all 'know' many things. I knew without the background knowledge of brain-gained experience, I knew from inside; the same 'inside' that I described earlier, my Soul (my sixth sense, my intuition, my source of inner teaching and consequent knowledge.)

My Soul recognised the off balanced person, because it knew that the partnership in the mind of that person was not equal, the two elements, the two parts of a human mind, the mortal brain and the immortal Soul were not in harmony, in balance in the mind. Does that surprise you? Well it surprises me, for no-one taught me that I had a Soul, let alone that it had a purpose which could be defined and a modus operandi that I should know about in order to make the most of this opportunity I have given myself to take a trip on the life ride once again.

I was taught well enough about my physical parts and organs, very little about my brain, I can see why now. The brain is just another power house, enormously complicated I know and baffling in its complexities, the complex engine of our human bodies, the part that makes every tiny thing about us function. That is what it does, it facilitates function of everything we can physically recognise, and those other things that we see the results of, in particular the processes like memory, recognition, evaluation, thought. Now everything gets much harder to understand (no wonder I was not taught much about the brain) for we really have no way of knowing, let alone proving much at all about the mind, the most amazing yet perplexing product of our brains. Luckily for me at this point in time, those facts are a distinct advantage. In the absence of any proof to the contrary I can weave my theories and pursue my ideas without much contradiction; although many others may believe differently there is nothing in my learning that proves to me that my beliefs are categorically wrong. They can neither be proved to be right or wrong, which fact serves to give value to them, at least in my eyes. I'd like not to be alone in this.

So, can I gather up the threads of my meandering thoughts to weave them into something concrete? Of course not, how can the non-physical become physical? Well in principle I guess it cannot, in the simplest of understandings what we see, is, and what we don't see, is not. Yet we all know that that is not the case. We don't see the wind but we see the result of its presence, we see the grasses rippling in a breeze, the trees doubling in a gale and the waves crashing in a storm, by these things we know the wind exists, but still we do not see it; we never see the wind itself. We feel the wind, our skin senses the quality it brings, warm and balmy to the skin, icy cold searing the tears from our eyes or singing its sounds round ears and chimney pots; but still we cannot see it. You need not think too deeply to realize there are many things we believe exist that we never actually see.

Can you touch the wind? In blindness there is no sight, but touch gives form to the things we, who see, take for granted. There is no form in the wind that we can know it through touch but we know it exists for it touches us. We see where it has been when it passes in a rage, for a trail of destruction is left in its wake. The last few days here have brought the 'Iris wind'. It comes most years just as the proud stems of my plants stand tall enough to show off their magnificent blooms. What happens? Up steps the wind to rag and jag those fragile, beautiful petals and beat the stems to the ground. The non physical (PHYSICAL *of matter, material* MATTER *that which has mass and occupies space* MATERIAL *concerned with the matter*) wind has had enormous effect on the matter of my irises and this I can see in the material form. I am in no doubt whatsoever that the wind exists for look what it has done, physical damage, even destruction. I can see the results of its presence; more than that, I can feel them. Not just the effects of its touching, hair standing on end, blue nose, sand in your eyes, skirt round your ears (why does that picture of Marilyn Monroe hover here?) nor, those very real, visible, plausible, physical effects of something very definitely non-physical: for me gazing on the iris bed, another consequence, emotion.

EMOTION *disturbance of mind.* (We are back full circle to disturbance of mind, but can I disregard this at the moment? I feel uncertain that I have finalised my belief about the true nature of mind, though I do confirm a disturbance of something.) *..mental sensation or state.* (Can I disregard mental etc also, for exactly the same reasons as before?) *..instinctive feeling as opposed to reason.* That I confirm wholeheartedly. Emotion is instinctive.

What exactly do we mean by instinctive? Perhaps I should say what do we understand by instinctive? INSTINCTIVE *innate propensity to certain seemingly rational acts performed without conscious intention.* What a mouthful, if you are any the wiser after reading that description then please fill me in. Whatever this thing we call instinct is, it is another of those inner qualities that are accepted as normal, acknowledged as usual even necessary parts of our human beingness. Yet where is this inner place that emanates these inner things? Do we automatically answer, in the mind? If so we are back where we started, accepting something that we cannot see, touch, taste, smell or hear in the literal sense. With all five of our known physical senses we cannot experience our minds, but we know it exists. Why is that? Because as with the wind, there are physical signs, signs left about for us to experience which demonstrate the presence of mind and which lead us to believe in it. The evidence leads us to our belief, our truth. The truth is we all have mind, we know and therefor acknowledge the fact. We also know that mind, like the wind and everything else in the universe, is composed of energy; nothing else, just energy.

That's a thought that has always fascinated me, and of course I don't understand it scientifically; but in terms of these invisible things (forces, some might say, FORCE *strength, power, impetus*) it is very easy to understand, for they somehow give form to the invisible. To know that the constituents of this nothing are described as power, force and impetus, fills the nothingness with body (and a strong one at that) and aptly describes both the wind and the mind. It does nothing to teach me the origin of the energy of mind. Could it, like the wind be the resulting energy of certain sets of circumstances, and like the variables in the energy that we know as wind, could mind energy vary according to the gathered conditions that prevail at any given time? That may describe in dilute form the birth of energy, but does nothing to show me where the mind energy is delivered from. Are you shouting that it must come from the brain? Why must it? We know some does, but must it all?

No-one has seen this creation created, no proud father has the video of this arrival, no-one has dyed the mind and watched its progress through the human form; I think if we could we would be in for a few surprises. You see, I believe that mind has another dimension to it which I am not convinced could possibly come from the very mechanistic organ that we know the brain to be: of course that we will never know unless someone volunteers the live inspection of a brain in action! Even that would teach us very little, as a brain functioning under such clinical conditions as would allow inspection would naturally be working very unnaturally (if you see what I mean.) Thus while mankind exists there will never be accurate and full knowledge of the workings of the human brain and in consequence no picture of mind. That is a thought

Soul Listening

which stops me in my tracks, so I will stop for now.

Another day and I sit respectfully in front of the light that is this computer's screen, sipping my morning rejuvenator, and looking at the keys which I'm waiting to start tapping on. I've glanced at the few lines above, the place I stopped yesterday. They have no familiarity as I read them for the first time; they hold no thought train or patterns for me to take up, to resume where I left off. Each time I have come to perform my promised daily (but in reality, not so daily) hour it has been like this, but very quickly I have found myself tapping, rarely glancing up and always wondering when I do, why on earth I am writing the words that I see I am. Yet some time later, as I'm feeling that it is time to pack up for the day, I have another peep at the screen and am always surprised. Yes, the trust I employ is not complete, (though I work at it) so I remain to some degree or another surprised and usually delighted by the way things seem to come round in full circle, leaving me not puzzled at the day's starting point but more marvelling at the outcome.

I've just read that first paragraph of the day as no tapping was forthcoming. I know that in there is a profound life lesson; if only I was clever enough to spell it out to you. Today it would seem there is nothing coming from without me, or through me, and to keep going with this it feels as though I have to use an entirely different method. Already I see that I am constantly checking the screen, not just to see what I am writing, but specifically to see where I have got to within that. Looking to see shows me what this is all about. It is about where I have 'got to'. That means where I have 'got to' on as many levels as I care to look and on as many levels as I can understand or translate that.

My family have taken enough notice (sarcasm, a 'nasty habit') to ask me if I have nearly finished the book and I have had to answer that "I have no idea." I suspect that was received as cantankerous, evasive, though it was nothing of the kind, for I have no way of knowing how much or how little there is to be written. I tried to explain that I was simply tapping and had no personal plan, plot, format, whatever.

*I 'received' the title as soon as I determined to have a go at something that had been no more than one of those ideas of mine, the ones that grew occasionally to a tiny bit more than an idea, when they were accompanied by some scribbled pages, notes, diagrams and sometimes illustrations. I thought that if ever I got into print my analogous writings would be accompanied by humorous drawings; you've probably noticed that not a lot of these things are to be seen in this work.

tappers note: original title 'From there to here in search of my Soul' later understood as guidance for the format.

Going with Soul

Having heard of these past pathetic attempts it was not surprising that I was seen as awkward and evasive in my answers, though I was very confident in telling them that I would tap on till the end and that I would know when the end was in sight.

My daughter looked at a print-out of this as far as it went some weeks ago. She is an avid reader and will devour anything and everything that comes her way. Reading this was no mean achievement as it looked like a toilet roll, yards of words, little in the way of punctuation; gaps, spelling mistakes, nonsense words and strange inserts in caps (where I had forgotten to release the key and of course had not seen the oversized words until they arrived on the paper.) It did strike me then that there would be an awful lot of hard work, particularly as I have no real computer know how, to get this lot into a form that could be offered to a publisher. That was only a little passing worry as the conditioned mind, that still exerts it's negative power at times, told me loud and clear that nobody was going to want to read my meanderings and that it was probably no more than something I had to get out of my system.

That was the best thing it could have said, as I have learnt that getting things out of ones system, in the right way, is the best thing anyone can do for themselves. The value of the cathartic experience is well documented. CATHARTIC *effecting catharsis.* CATHARSIS *outlet to emotion afforded by drama, etc. or by abreaction* and now I see where today's apparently strange beginning has brought us. We have come to the outlet of emotion. EMOTION *instinctive feeling as opposed to reason.* Are these things, instinctive feelings that come to our minds produced by the engine, the motor of the brain machine? Doesn't the word instinctive suggest something that comes with us into this world? So, where does it come from? How does instinct get into our minds? How does it come with us? Does it come from our brains? Isn't the brain grown in the womb along with every other part of us? Isn't it all new, un-used and un-worked? Where and when does all this inner stuff, intuition, instinct, inner knowledge and inner wisdom get into our minds? How is it that we arrive in the world with emotions? Where, when and how do those become part of the new-born's luggage? Has the brain picked up all this in the womb and filled our minds already? WHAT EXACTLY IS MIND, specifically how is the energy that is mind, formed? What are the constituents of mind energy? Above all and of paramount importance to these writings, WHAT EXACTLY ARE EMOTIONS? (see above).

But for a moment back to my daughter and her reading achievements. She didn't really make a comment after she had scanned (for at her speed I think scan is more apposite than read) this document, so with drooping voice I forced myself to ask, "Well, what do you think, is it worth me going on with it?" You'll notice in this the loss of trust on my side in the great power of my

Soul Listening

Soul, yet another tick for the ego in fear-mode. Truth is this does keep happening. I've spent so long in this unbalanced state that each time I voice some success in that department (achieving better balance between body, and all contained therein, and Soul, and all contained therein) fear, in any one of it's guises, girds it's loins for a full frontal attack of previously unfelt ferocity.

It's like anyone losing their grip on a situation, somehow there is always just that bit more strength to be mustered when the end of a battle is looming. Not that I envisage an end to my balancing act, the future is not mine to know; from experience I know there has been just one more bridge to cross each time I think that I have successfully negotiated, what appeared at the time to be, the last one in sight. From that I conjecture more bridges, mountains, battles, however you want to describe the events that lead us to enlightenment; but I view them without fear, for each one is easier to cross, climb or win. What I see when I stop to look back is a definite improvement in my human condition as I dispense with a heavy cloud of fear and replace it with the light of Unconditional Love. The more times I am able to do this the more faith I have in the process. I know now that however wobbly my wavering, however far I sometimes feel that I have strayed from my convictions, the contact that I have made with my Soul is so alive and well that I will always hear it's voice and be drawn back to its ways. Its way seems to me to be to be solely advantageous to my human existence.

But, back to that story line again, where my needy ego was needing a stroke, (how I look forward to the day when it doesn't, and just in case you wonder about it's role, it's purpose then, well, all I can say for now is that I have great plans for it.) It didn't get one, but neither was it whacked. "Well, it's OK mum, but where's it leading; it feels as though it should be going somewhere and it isn't yet?"

This comment has really brought me up to date, still being led and still certain of going somewhere. In many senses there is no punch line, no neat rounding off, no spectacle at the end of the road for me to dazzle your vision with, for my road and yours goes on without end, my journey and yours takes place whether we are conscious of that journey or not. I am conscious (reminder: aware, knowing) now of the never ending cycles and circles of life and even more aware that what I have been trying to tell you has no beginning and no end. I have covered a few miles on a circular bus tour and taken you with me between some of the stops. We've waited and watched, sometimes we've wandered off and sometimes we've stood as a bus went by; but it matters not, for wherever and however we move around the circle it truly has no beginning and no end and as you dwell on that the idea of infinity and the infinite universe begins to make some sense. In a way there is no leaving a circuitous journey, however large or small the cycle, whether so unimaginably vast that we never see it all or so small that we pass the same spot many times, it makes no difference. There is no place to leave the circle as it has no end, no break; no gap to squeeze through and leave by. 'Stop the world I want to get off' would seem the only way, yet that step would be just another one around your Soul's infinite cycle. You and I are just passing along, passing through a certain place at a certain time and we will both keep on going on. That seems to me a wonderful prospect, one that I cannot reason or understand in an intelligent, rational way, but one that I fully comprehend through my emotions, that is to say, through my Soul. Through my Soul the emotional concept of this immortal circle of travel and enlightenment is making my physical being fizzy with the excitement of it all; through my mortal brain, which lacks the scientific grasp and theoretical understanding of the infinite universe, my physical body feels a bit sick and my mind feels a bit fearful.

I am conscious once more of being by the roadside of my journey and that I have brought you here too. Are you asking, like my daughter, "Well, where's it all leading? Why are we here? What has she brought us here for? What is there to see?" I will look around now we are here and tell you what I have become aware of; I will offer it with the nearest thing to Unconditional Love that I know and with the deepest trust I have learned.

Episode Three
Soul Listening

This is what I am conscious of, here and now, Soul Listening.

As the title of my story suggests, you have been with me on the part of my life's journey which took me from there (I guess that's where it started) to here. I was searching for my Soul, there, even though I was not aware of doing so: that's the beauty of it, even without any nurture, care or attention it gives its all. Think then, as I do constantly, how much, much more 'all' there is to be had with just a little nurture, care or attention from you. If you can conceive of such wonders, try to imagine the joy to be had from giving even half the attention to our Souls that we give to our negative minds.

I was there searching and now I am here with you, now I am not searching. I am so conscious of my Soul (conscious as before, literally meaning aware, knowing) that the rest of my journey can be made in some peace, come what may.

As I begin to write the rounding off for you I am totally stopped in my tracks. I have been aware that what I had to offer you in terms of the amount of words in this book was nearing its conclusion, and with that feeling I began to think how and what the last section would be. I knew as soon as I shut down yesterday that I must call it Soul Listening.

This was given to me over two years ago, when the Soulcards came into my possession and I began to realise the incredible power for change that they offered, both in my own life and the lives of others. I thought then that my work as a therapist was taking off, so to offer my services I decided the most 'business-like' way was to have informative leaflets printed. It was early days, and I had little idea then what could be achieved through making acquaintance with one's Soul, the only thing I knew, without any doubt at all, was that it was necessary to listen, and when I listened, I heard the words, Soul Listening. That was the 'work' I offered, and those words, to me, looked beautiful on the outside of a tasteful leaflet. Not beautiful enough evidently, for although I placed them, in what I thought were the right outlets, in towns and villages within a fourteen mile radius, the response was slow. Oh, all right then, it was virtually non-existent, and that was a blow, a real downer (I think that's the idiom.) The second lot of leaflets I had printed were on much cheaper paper! I was giving up! Then, as always, every time I reached that state something happened to push me back on the track. There were responses from people looking for help from their Souls. Every few months, when ideas of abandoning my thoughts and theories were paramount, a weary traveller would arrive at my door; sometimes in response to the known offer of Soul help, but more often in a strange round-a-bout way. Interestingly without being previously aware of my involvement in Soul work and my use of the power of the Soul no-one protested at that; surprisingly and if I am honest, humblingly (definitely not in the dictionary, but you know what I mean) they seemed to know they had a Soul. Everyone indicated the same area of their body as its home: to think it had taken me over fifty five years to find mine! The help and healing we always received was astounding. Can I say it, please? It was to me miraculous sometimes. Astounding would have kept me on the road, the other left me leaping along it.

Do you know, when I was thinking that it was beginning to feel as though I would be writing the last section of this book by myself, and as I became more certain that that would be the case, I never had it in my mind to tell you any of what I have just tapped. Today I was initially stopped from telling you about Soul Listening, by a thick cotton-wool sensation in that part of my head normally occupied by my brain, which let no thoughts or words through. I sat getting into a bit of a tizz glaring at the non-moving script before me, glaring none too good-naturedly. All I could see were three groups of words that had come up in caps, again. I'll give them to you now, as I only managed to get tapping past them when I had completely acknowledged them. They hold great significance for me. SOUL LISTENING.....THIS....I AM.....I AM NOT SEARCHING. It wasn't so easy accepting those words. I knew exactly what they were telling me, at my Soul level, but I had so got it into my head that now it was my turn, I would show you what I could do, I would finish this document off in style, my style. It was me who had always wanted to write a book wasn't it? At last I was going to get a look in, pull all the threads together and leave you gasping at the way I wove them all so skilfully together into the wondrous web that illustrated so sparklingly my theory of Soul Listening. But no matter how I searched it was not there, not one word. Of course not; there can be no ego stroking in Soul Listening. I (of the balanced mind) don't need it. The moment I knew that the old fingers started to fly over the keys, bashing out spelling mistakes as rapidly as usual. So tomorrow I shall listen to my Soul, stop searching, and peep with anticipation at the outcome.

There was no tomorrow here for that yesterday. It is now February 2001, I'm back.

Well you weren't aware that I had ever been away, and once again in the traditional sense I have not been, though I have been away from this for a very long time. The last date I sat here, keeping my pact to write for an hour a day come what may, was late June or early July 2000, so long ago I'm barely sure. May came, silently, stealthily, as ever from behind to make absolutely certain of approaching unseen. No time to take avoidance actions, no opportunity to see and prepare for what lay ahead. May, or more correctly LIFE, caught up with me as it is won't to do with each and every one of us. At that moment it wasn't so much that my good intentions, my promises to self and silent prayer to dear departed one were forgotten, far from it; it was that they could no longer find their way to the top of my priorities heap. It's at such times I long to halt the relentless race of hands round the time-dial of my life, either that or have the capacity to wind myself into such a frenzy of activity that I watch in awe as the fast-forward video of my days, weeks or months, plays itself out in a matter of hours, leaving the rest of those days, weeks and months for me to savour and fill with meaningful delights. But life is not like that, and you hardly need me to remind you. Perhaps I'm just re-confirming it for my own benefit, I remain ever hopeful that there is potential in life to do more than just get through it. To some that may seem a depressing outlook to have, the 'just getting through it', others, sadly, know exactly the feelings and the experiences that lead to such a view.

My view, when I left you at the beginning of the summer last year, was that I was, at long, long last getting somewhere, at the very least I had seen the heading displayed before me here, SOUL LISTENING. Reading that gave me a lift. I sensed it as the third and final part of this story, more than that, I believed at that time that it was the part that I would be able to tell for myself. I believed I had a pretty good idea what Soul Listening was and that I was in a position to tell you all. At the deeper personal level it looked to me as though for the very first, that's the ONLY time in my life to date, I was going to get to the finishing post; to make a dream, my own dream for myself alone, become reality. DREAM *have visions, etc.....*VISION *imaginative insight.....* Is this the clue to what happened to me then? At the time when I was beginning to believe in myself, just as I was convincing myself that at least one of those things that I had set my sights on (to write a book) was in fact a real possibility and not, as I was told as a child of doubtless boundless imagination, a pipe-dream, 'reaching for the stars'. Set in the purely practical realms of my upbringing this would not have been perceived as even a vaguely achievable dream.

Looking back I don't recall much that was agreed to be possible or available to me, certainly my imaginings, my visions, my dreams were decidedly beyond the stars; or so I was told, and being a good child I accepted the conditioning, which has rested uneasily with my being ever since. But rested (or as it has felt, firmly lodged, even embedded) it has for almost sixty years. For only recently have I been able to see clearly the particular, personal pattern of my conditioning; the many times of having the finishing post, the winning line, the goal, not just in view but so nearly within my grasp, only to drop it. I feel quite foolish now that I can clearly see what has been happening: how was it I couldn't see this before? My answer to the feeling stupid me is that conditioning, or the negative mind I speak about, is absolute; it is so powerful that it forms a mindset, rather like an over-ride button which is permanently poised to come on. My answer to the not seeing lies in exactly the same place.

Once again the mind has come to the forefront of my reasoning. The negatively conditioned mind, yours and mine, is such an awesome thing; so strong in its position as driver of the body we inherit that it can and mostly does railroad completely that other part of the human being, the Soul. It was only when I began to listen to my Soul that I was able to start the process that led me to see, after so long living the mistakes of my fearful conditioned mind, that my imagination, my dreams, my vision were, and are, real for me. They do not stem from my conditioned mind, though I have to pursue them there with the faculties of brain endowed by my parentage, my ancestral lineage and my upbringing.

The birth place of my dreams is my Soul. My Soul; the seat of emotions, the source of dreams and visions, creativity in fact. So as I come to hear and accept the things my Soul tells me so I come to understand that many of the things I had previously heard and accepted (conditioning) were not gems from my Soul. They came from the beliefs and well-wishing of others in charge of my development but they by no means reflected me. Me (and you too.) ME, *see I....I*, well, my dictionary tells me that I is me! I think that takes me back to square one. I look at I on the screen and see one.(1) That's it, me equals one: from my perspective (searching for me) that equates with 'the one'. Now to those defining words again and I see ONE *subject or object of self - consciousness*. Aha! CONSCIOUSNESS *total of a persons thoughts and feelings*. Yes I thought so! If you can allow my substitution of the word emotions here for the word feelings (as explained below) Me can be defined in total as thoughts and emotions. I wonder if you agree? I hope you follow the reasoning. Therefor Me should be found, available for inspection as it were, in my mind, through my thoughts (products of my brain) and emotions (products of my Soul.) But what if Me (or you) has been conditioned, as I know we have all been to some lesser or greater degree, conditioned through our learning experiences to function with negative thoughts? Sometimes so many or such strong negative mind-sets that we never really hear our emotions, never really know them? What is the Me that we then experience, the Me by which we are driven along our individual life paths? Is this perhaps not a true Me at all but a half Me; an incomplete Me out of touch with those positive emotions of the creative Soul?

Now as I told you yesterday it's a long time since I was last here tapping away, and as I've yet to read my story, as told through these 'tappings', I'm not certain that I put my ideas about the difference between feelings and emotions to you. Either way it seems called for at this juncture. It has been my experience that the 'feelings' we describe as 'having' whether anger, fear, misery, etc. or happiness, joy, etc. are actually experienced in our bodies as real, 'concrete', physical things, (I call them symptoms) changes in our bodies that alert our minds to our physical sensations. Our brain records the symptoms; it alerts us to the fact that some-where in our bodies we are experiencing a feeling. We feel it, hence feelings.

If you have ever had to sit still for a long time when what you would rather do is stand up, move about, leap and shout, you start to experience physical feelings/symptoms. The frustration, the impatience or the annoyance that sit with those feelings are emotions. But what alerts you to the emotions? Is it some abstract, intangible thing? No, it's the tingling bum cheeks, the itching feet, the aching back, and you squirm. Your body displays your feelings to you with physical realities. No-one would call these bodily symptoms emotions would they? No, I think we can agree that they are feelings, which I presume the brain triggers into motion to wake us up to the emotions we are experiencing. So pursuing that line of reasoning, why does the brain organise these sensations within the physical body? It would seem it is causing physical discomfort (in the cases of positive emotions it causes physical bliss!) for no other reason than to alert us to the fact that we are 'having an emotion'. Why, if emotion emanates from the brain, would it need to go to such enormous lengths with that multitude of arousal symptoms that we are all familiar with, solely for the purpose of having the cognitive areas of aforesaid amazing organ recognise from the bodily sensations it has just constructed (feelings) that it has emotions? It would be a foregone conclusion, wouldn't it? It does not seem logical to me that the brain is the source of emotions. May I offer you my belief that feelings are the physical symptoms of emotions; they manifest in every single part of our human body, brain included.

I feel that I am now back to square one (yes, again!) faced with the prospect of trying to define mind. Impossible? I hope not, for if I cannot succeed in putting forward to you a theory that could possibly hold more than a drop of water, then I will have failed in my desire to spread the news of the power of your Soul. Having been listening to mine (in honesty it's been more trying to, struggling to at times) but having been doing that consciously now for three years, (come next month) I have come to know of Soul power and its value. I believe so firmly in it that, for the good of us all, I cannot fail.

That word brings me back to one of the great hurdles of my own existence, falling at the last fence. Well in case you never read this book I can tell you here and now that this is one finishing line I will be crossing. I can't of course tell you whether I will cross it first as a winner, or last, as the ultimate trier, but cross it I assure you I will.

You see, having listened and in doing that received the wisdom (for that read enlightenment, which is knowledge) of my Soul, I know that the only way for me to be, is to be true to Me. In listening to my Soul a process for finding Me has been given. It is slow at times and as some-one following this process reported, "painful" (I probably would at times have said "bloody painful") but it works, the Shadows rise and float away, the power of the Soul shines through ever more brightly, knowledge of Me and You floods in, in blinding flashes of enlightenment. No more need to question "what is enlightenment?" It is knowing yourself, finding You, building the total person; your complete Me. As you shed negative conditioning (which I still like to tell seekers are Soul Shadows) as you shake off the layers that do the real, new found You no favours at all, it is as if lights go on in the mind; things become so clear.

Clarity can only show itself in the light and those details that the dimmed forty watt puts in shaded corners simply have no place to hide any longer. Knowledge and realization appear as flashing lights to the mind and you 'see' all you want to see so clearly. It can be dazzling when that penny drops; when enlightenment is no longer a word of letters, meaningless letters to be chased through the lines of some-one else's words. You will sense a brighter outlook, feel the flow of your own power, know You, Your wisdom, Your creativity, Your dreams. It all becomes real, becomes possible, and in the truest physical sense you feel lighter, while your mind soars with the possibilities of your being, now you begin to discover the Me of you.

I see that we have returned again to the mind. You see the mind is the Me (and You.)

Knowing how much I have previously banged on about the fearful mind, the negative mind-set mind, the conditioned mind, you may find this statement as bewildering as I did when I looked up today to see where I had left myself yesterday. Actually where I found myself, when I set off on my round of daily duties, was in my mind constantly chewing over that phrase, 'the mind is the Me' and conversely 'the Me is the mind.' What a statement to have tapped. Well, I think I had always known that I am my mind, but I guess I had not had cause to ponder the true significance of this. It was the search for Me that led me to think more deeply, and the answer I found was not what I had hoped for. You see I knew the Me of my mind and I didn't much care for her. The Me I now sought was imagined to be, somehow in every respect, 'better' than that one so familiarly acquainted with. That 'better' one couldn't possibly be there living like a twin with the one I have been trying to depose could it? No, impossible, so where was Me? Yet it felt so right, though in all my deep thinking while I searched for Me I had not considered it to be so; but as the words played over and over in that needle-stuck groove of my brain I could feel my truth behind them. Enlightenment was mine; everything had simply, almost silently slotted into place for me; and at that moment the trepidation over my task, to tell you what mind is evaporated. Puff! Understanding! Clarity! Knowing! Everything that aids those moments of enlightenment were mine. My mind was heaving with the words that I knew would express so convincingly everything that was tumbling into place at that moment of truth, and I couldn't wait to climb the staircase to this computer to share it with you all.

Oh! if only enlightenment, which means nothing more ordinary than having the understanding to see things clearly, as they are in one's own truth, if only, if only.....if only it were an image that could be caught, frozen in time, forever. If only it could be so, I would have it here in front of me now, refer to it and simply translate the picture into words for you. But no, I have no picture, I have no sense of that delicious emotion, just the memory of feeling a thousand light bulbs click on simultaneously in the brain and the shedding light that sends the mind soaring. I think that's where joy is born, and in that state the body follows suite and suddenly joins in the experience of flying, rising above the mundane, leaving the niggling aches and pains of the everyday human body behind, far behind. On every level your brain can encompass it you feel lighter; true enlightenment.

In ...lighten...meant? MEAN *to have as one's purpose, for a purpose.* PURPOSE *object to be attained, thing intended.* Does that mean then that the thing intended, the purpose of each human being is to have light within? To become enlightened is to find the light inside? So simple and yet so difficult to express, for I felt, I knew, I had experienced a flash of said enlightenment, as we all do on occasions. But it was just that, it was a flash from my own inner light, impossible to capture and show to you. Yesterday, when it happened I was so certain of it, so sure I could hold on to it, so certain of it's validity, so sure of the breakthrough I had experienced, that I almost couldn't wait to come and tell you all about it. I guess that was the mistake I made; I should have found a way to record every detail of the event, because shortly after, when the phrase 'the Me is the mind' started to repeat itself again, the clouds had descended and the lights had all fused.

Soul Listening

I cannot describe the disappointment I felt or the trepidation today as I began my climb. However was I going to continue with the words tapped here yesterday? With hindsight I now know that I had lost contact with my Soul, not fuses blown at all, but a poor connection; my mind had slipped back into its lifelong fearful state, negative conditioning raised its ugly head and darkness temporarily blotted out the link I'm working at establishing with my Soul. I was beginning to make plans for the tapping, my ego ever hopeful of proving its worth, still poking in as it does however many times I remind myself that this is coming from the Soul and my imagination is not required. All that is required is just enough brain-power to make the machine obey my commands to place the letters into words.

So there I was starting the climb, feeling those old familiar feelings of failure and inadequacy. Forgotten was the joy I have experienced at each and every tapping session; the wondrous way that the words and sentences have been unfolding before me, for it has truly been like that. I make no plans, well only ever very briefly, on those bad, disconnected days. I come here with trust, complete trust that the things that my Soul require me to know or see or hear or share will come forth. They have done.

Sometimes I have an inkling of where we might be heading and I'm always wrong! Very often I'm surprised and wonder however what has been tapped can be appropriate, but I know that in a magical way, like the weaving of a thread through a garment, the thread will have a place and that the beginning and the end of that will be securely anchored where it belongs in that robe. At that point, without thought or decision and without reading through the lines I am given the feeling that that's it for the day and it is. I long ago learnt that if I want to hear the voice of my Soul I have to act on the feelings (those bodily feelings we were talking about earlier) and that's when I shut down the machine.

But to return to the story; a few steps up the staircase and there was a knock at the door. Two J.W.'s are standing, smiling in the path of the day's gusting rainstorm. I am, as always, amazed at their resilience, their determination and above all their faith. In a none too kind voice I might say "blind faith," but admiration for them I definitely have and in the general manner of my own doctrine of 'live and let live' I smile encouragingly; after all they may have something new to say today. My true thoughts are "I wonder why they make the trek all the way down our muddy pot-holed drive, in this weather? They've been so many times and know that I am an unlikely convert; they also know some of my views which firmly contradict their own teachings." We have a short exchange and they smile farewell through blinded raindrop glasses. I begin my climb again, puzzling over that brief encounter. I puzzle over everything now, every picture no matter how large or how small, how ever vivid or, as in this case, however blurred; for it is my belief that every single thing that takes place around me is an opportunity to learn. Blowed if I could see anything at all to learn from that event!

So I opened up and there were those words 'the mind is the Me' and I was paralysed. My mind looped the loop, where could I go from here? It seemed nowhere, there was no tapping forthcoming, but negative thoughts came aplenty. To think only the other day I had all the positivity to proclaim my race won; in my mind's eye at that stage I could literally see that finishing tape, and now, foiled, stuck in the old negative mind-set nothing was flowing, no words to tap at all. No thoughts that I could muster in that frame of mind rang with any sense of truth or conviction at all, the creativity, the purpose all gone. I admit to you a feeling of panic (that would have been an excellent time to do a bit of Soul work on myself, on that Shadow which I would love to enlighten) until I suddenly saw again the light in that J.W.'s smile.

Well, I know that they come with love, but on a day like today, to visit me, did they come with Unconditional Love? I suppose while having such thoughts, thinking fondly, even gratefully of two of my fellow human beings my mind was gradually reforming a stronger connection with my Soul. I was slipping out of my mind's childhood conditioning and establishing once again a stronger link with the positive offerings of my Soul. Suddenly I could hear my own voice repeating some of the words that I had offered in conversation on the doorstep, and a few hundred watts shone into my mind, and in the beam of that light the picture offered to me by my visitors became crystal clear. I'm going to repeat that to you here and now, as my feeling is that I have been given a second chance to describe to you a true incidence of my own enlightening process.

Recall if you will that when I first 'looked' at the picture I could 'see' nothing at all of significance. I was at that time of 'looking' functioning in a negative (honestly I was a bit judgemental) state. I only recalled to mind the important part of the picture (in this case my words, which I am coming to, be patient please) when my state of mind was positive (I'd rather call that loving, the unconditional variety.) The words I heard were in response to a question about God. Basically I think, without misquoting them, that they believe that God will save the earth and save mankind with it. I told them that I did not believe in God as a being, rather I believed that God (if we must use that word) is energy, an essence from which we humans have developed. As such we all carry within us (somewhere) a drop, or drops or parts of that essence or energy. I believe that energy to be a powerful creative force for good, the energy of Unconditional Love, an energy 'carried' in our Souls to be used to save ourselves and our beautiful world, rather than destroying it (as we undoubtedly are.) I told them we could do that; that we do have the potential to do the 'saving' that they seem quite happy to expect of God.

"If you don't believe in a God who is going to save us, do you believe in evil, in the Devil? " "No, I don't, but 'evil' is within us all, or more correctly, the potential for living in ways which are completely the opposite of living within the orb of Unconditional Love, are inherent to us all."

There was more along those lines, not necessary to repeat here, for the point I am trying to illustrate is not about what was said or the implications of the words, their value or invalidity; it is not about trying to make a point or putting things across to another, it is not about how my ideas were received or not received. The importance of this interlude, this vignette of vision in a life of pictures, is that for a while I could see nothing really worth looking at, even though a small voice had alerted me to look, I still saw nothing of any significance to me. Then as I was gradually able to move my mind into a more balanced state, that means to me that I was moving from the judgemental state of my conditioning into being more in touch with the 'unconditionally loving' state of my Soul, I saw the picture anew and the message for me to see was no longer obscured by the darkness of that described mind state. It was illuminated I believe by the loving desire of my Soul that I should be given the opportunity to learn a little more about the true Me.

In a way the words that I heard, which I had offered my callers, were not new to me; they were echoes of the thoughts I have been exploring, testing, rejecting and re-avowing, time after time during the last three years of learning how to be with my Soul. As I said before, the actual words by themselves were not important; the important thing was the realisation after the event. The part of this exchange that brought enlightenment at that moment was that, for the first time in all the long and often lonely months of experimenting with my theories, for the very first time I was able to hear my own beliefs loud and clear. I heard some of the truths that are mine. Hopefully not mine alone, but definitely in that instance solely mine, for although the two J. W's listened politely I knew, while offering my thoughts, that this was not the way they viewed the set-up. Most definitely not, nor was it in the religious sense the way I was brought up. I was hearing myself, hearing a truth which at that particular moment was not part of any-one else's truth, just mine, and in that case part of me; and so, as I recalled the events on my doorstep, I knew that another small part of (the mind of) Me had been illuminated.

I received a little more enlightenment and a surge of emotion (an emotion that at this time I do not have description of) comes to my countenance and I smile. Actually I've not looked at myself at such times, but thinking of it now I know I most probably have a silly self-satisfied grin accompanying my anticipation for what is to come next on this great adventure. It seems great to me; a journey of constant discovery and surprises. Even the painful ones can be faced with hopeful expectancy for, by working with the Soul's healing process, I know that every Shadow lifted into consciousness can be enlightened, no matter how dense and dark that Shadow might be. If it is felt, acknowledged and then is given the light of the Soul it becomes lighter. Then lighter and even lighter until it is no longer a Shadow. As the Shadows are removed more space is created for the light to fill.

Are you asking, "but what is this light she is going on about, and where are the shadows?" I don't blame you for that, I am also always asking questions and often finding other people's way of seeing things very hard to follow. It is very difficult trying to teach ideas to others. I know that I've said this before, but I think it can take a repeat; many, many times on my journey I have found it impossible to understand what people think they have discovered. How could I 'let go', I didn't know what it meant, I had no concept, no understanding, no experience of what it meant to let go, so how could I possibly do that? I couldn't. How could I 'love myself'? I didn't know how to, so how could I? I didn't. How could I 'go with the flow'? I couldn't see any flow, so how could I go with one? I didn't. I felt enormously frustrated by the books and people who had this ability, this secret knowledge to do all these things I was being told to do; I felt cross that I was being denied these magic passports to the kingdom of happiness that I was seeking. Was there a secret society? How could I get the password?

I am acutely aware that through all this rambling I may not have conveyed a jot of practical advice to you, but keep going, it is coming. What I hope I have been sharing with you is a process; the way in which my journey through a very ordinary life as an ordinary human being has led me to something I believe is extra-ordinary (to say the least.) How even more extra-ordinary it would be if the sharing of my very small trek across our huge planet was to take you to the place I want to tell you about. A place where you too can begin the process of finding balance, achieving wholeness, one-ness, happiness, whatever it is that seems to be your, as yet unattainable, life goal.

To convey, to impart, to communicate; what I think that means is to teach; which is something that does not sit too comfortably on my shoulders. To teach something that is unknown, not proven, that feels to me how it does when people call me a 'healer.' I am not a healer: should anyone make that claim? I believe we heal ourselves by acknowledging the help of others (in my case the 'other' is my Soul.) A 'healer' acts as a catalyst for change within another person, the vital element in this exchange is Unconditional Love, no healing can take place without that being present. Methods, practices, aids, therapists, whatever guise the healing takes place beneath, these are simply tools we seem to need to make the process acceptable to our poor conditioned minds. They are not necessary. All that is required is access to the energy of Unconditional Love. All that is needed is a Soul, yours, mine, anyone's; we all have one, they come as part of the human package, they are a free gift.

Funny how we rifle the world for the free gift, something for nothing, it's the reason we are all in the dreadful state we find ourselves now. Yet we need look no further than within, for within each and every person who chooses to walk a path of life on earth is the most valuable free gift you could ever imagine. I want you to know about it, that's all. Then it's up to you. It is your free gift, I've got mine, and right now I need to use it to climb this stumbling block I am experiencing over teaching resonating within the same space as healing.

You see I know I am not a healer though healing takes place in my presence. I insist that I am not a healer; those words are my truth. My belief in these situations is that healing will be given and received through the energy of the Unconditional Love of the Souls present from the power and the might of the all-encompassing Universal Soul (pure goodness, or God if you wish.) Healing is always given and always received. It may be we witness a miraculous change, it may be less significant, but I believe and trust, therefor I know that it is appropriate for the situation. I never hope for more, nor look to the possibility of less. I trust implicitly in the wisdom of Soul and acknowledge that the help given comes from the Universal Soul, the source of Unconditional Love. If one of the helping Souls in question is mine that is wonderful for me, I admit it. I am human, and only starting out on the road to balance; but teaching? Well that is still an idea that feels housed in a state of imbalance though I have had the opportunity of some enlightenment on that. Can I tell you a couple of things, little exchanges in my days that allowed me to 'listen' and then to 'see' what was being offered on the subject? I hope I can recall clearly enough for you to understand how the 'hearing' and then 'seeing' process works within for me, for my enlightenment, my understanding, my guidance if I want it. I always do want it, I ask for it and I am thankful for it and I make that known in silent (and sometimes not so silent) thanks to the Universal Soul, who I know has to work very hard lighting up my own in order that it is operational through all its Shadows.

I am very lucky to have a couple of disciples, without whom I could well have fallen into the ditch at the side of my roadway and happily stayed there, lying on my back watching the skies above in an uncomfortable, but non the less acceptable, sort of peaceful solitude. Even more of a blessing is their complete trust in me and my Soul; because of this our Soul work together is a joy. When one of them told me after her last visit that she would be back soon I felt surprised and heard myself say that she did not need me, she could 'do it' herself.

Soul Listening

That led to the recounting of a difficult time in her life when she felt desperate enough to seek some help from her doctor: he would not agree to prescribe for her, telling her that she could get better by herself. Once more I felt surprised; this stayed with me, as did my own and the doctor's strangely similar words.

A picture for me, as every exchange and experience can be every moment of every day if we wish it. We don't have the time! We don't notice the pictures! If we recall the incidents we don't realise they are significant; all these things. So it was quite a while later in the day when I acknowledged my replays of the conversation and most importantly, the emotions that accompanied the picture; two incidences of surprise. At last I woke up to co-operate with my Soul which had desperately been trying to gain my attention. You see it will always do that, and once you begin to listen to it you will find that the listening gets easier; I mean after three years it only took me half a day and two pictures!! No come back, don't put the book down, I'm only being truthful. It has not been and still is not simple for me, but it's worth it, it really works if you give it a chance, and like anything new to you the more you practice the easier it becomes. I really believe that soon it will become second nature to me and I won't have to make any effort to think about it at all. I was surprised, an emotion to be looked at, and as I did this I realised that I did not think that the doctor was right to say 'she could do it'. How could she when he had not explained what it was she had to do, or how it could be done? I thought it wrong of him. I made a judgement of him, without knowing anything more than the few words that had been passed on to me. If I could judge him on that, how much easier it was to make judgement on my own words, "You can do it yourself." How unkind of me. She had said she wanted to come again, that was her truth and I had over-ruled it. In my ego keenness to have my theories proven I was looking to her as a keen follower to take up my baton and run with it. I was listening to myself in my fearful mind, my Soul was overshadowed again. I was looking to some-one else to prove me right, if you like to make it all come right for me, to justify me. Only I can justify Me, Me is for me to find, then build, she has her Me to grow.

So what was that picture all about? I knew at that moment that I had to teach her how to use her own Soul, I had no right to expect that she could just do it, I hadn't properly taught her and so she couldn't; simply that. If I am holding something of any true value to any one other than myself then I have to try and teach what I believe to be the truth; if it has any value I have to impart its wisdom in a way that it can be understood. So I phoned. Well actually she phoned me, (talk about being given another chance to get it right, so I gave thanks) and I said "sorry" and of course I'd love her to come when she needs to, and no, I shouldn't have said "you can do it, because I have not made it clear to you how you are able to."

Next day I went to a workshop, to be taught how to teach by experiencing some-one doing just that (which naturally I didn't realise at the time, but, yes, please believe me, the light dawned before I got home!) The day was advertised as Soul Song, a day in a nearby church, spent with a soprano who lives locally, (although she sings world-wide) and her friend, a composing musician. The aim: to show us the way to discover our own voices, of the singing variety that is, previous ability or knowledge of singing not required. That and the title seemed to me to be too much of an opportunity to let pass by.

I have always warbled, it has come as second nature to me to open the mouth and strum the vocal chords. My mother was often trilling away, I guess I just followed suit, it was accepted as the thing to do. Later on, continuing the tradition, I trilled away constantly in the privacy of my own home. Unfortunately my own home, as I thought of it, was not my own in the true sense of the word; it was a joint, shared home and the husband I was sharing it with, as you may recall, was a most troubled man. (What I really want to call him is a troubled soul; I thought of him as such, way back then when Soul was an unconsciously and infrequently used word in my vocabulary.) To put it bluntly, and a little more politely than he did, he thought I made the most ghastly noise which drove him to distraction; a state of being that was definitely, for my safety, not advisable.

Unfortunately, things we adopt during our so-called formative years (can I call them in-formative or de-formative?) have staying power and for a long time it was almost a reflex action to open up and make a noise. Thinking back I'm sure the singing (I insist on calling it that, after all the music practice and aural exams I took my reasonable diagnosis of the sound that came forth is that it bore much more resemblance to sweet trilling than the noises of a night-time cat wail) came as a response to good things. You know the sort I mean; the shine of your child's hair as you brush it at the start of a new day, the snowy gleam of purity as the first snowdrop catches a beam of winter sun light, the smell of the briny as the waves break in foam on a sparkle-washed beach . . . . stop me, I could go on for books and books. We all have lists of our own special pleasures, things that start that little bubble of something inside us all welling up to become happiness.

At welling times I burst into song. It wasn't that I wanted to incur wrath, but for a long long time I simply could not stop myself, despite the trouble that ensued. Gradually, that piece of positive, good for me conditioning became eroded; over a period of time I learnt just as those rats did who received an electric shock each time their behaviour was deemed incorrect. Slowly, but surely, I stopped singing. Many, many years later, when conditions seemed more favourable, I had a tentative try again but my children had received the childhood messages that mother could not sing, that in fact the noise she made was so dreadful it had to be banned. They were conditioned, they had seen and heard her punished for the offence and they tried to continue where their father had left off. I attempted some re-educating and I joined a local choir. Things were sweet for a while.

Then once again my circumstances, here meaning my important relationships (the place where Soul Shadows are mirrored and magnified for the opportunity to learn), changed for the worst. Well that's how I saw it then, before I got the Soul bug. Times were so difficult that the little bubbles did not turn into the sort of joy that had enough oomph to kick-start my former reaction, singing, into action. Silence fell again, and for a long time I quietly lamented that I had lost my singing voice, although I didn't stop to wonder why I could no longer sing. Naturally I did not hear my Soul telling me that I had lost my voice, I was not yet listening to it. Later, after a lot of Soul Listening, I discovered that people did not listen to me, (particularly and tellingly those closest to me.) As I continued listening to my Soul and looking at the pictures of my life as they were offered, I realised that I had never been listened to, therefor I was conditioned to expect not to be heard. Gradually I saw the nuts and bolts beneath this and understood that if you don't expect to be heard, that is, you have learned that you are not going to be heard, unconsciously you stop making any effort to be heard by any-one, self included; but that revelation came further down the line.

I stopped trying to be heard at a very, very young age! It was probably in this mode that I began to develop the habit of hearing others, which I soon honed to such a fine art that I never heard myself after that time; until that voice came out of the ether and told me that the cards I had just purchased were to be used for Soul Listening. As I see those words tapped across the screen I have the thought that if I had not grown up to hear others, rather than myself, I would never have heard that voice and certainly would have been far less willing to take heed of it. I did heed it, and eventually found that it was not just a message telling me how to advertise my 'card reading'. You will remember this did not take off, had it done so I doubt that I would have made any progress, for I would have revelled in the belief that I was helping others and never looked further than the ego stroking gained from that. I may have given some help to some people but that would not have helped me, the real Me I sought.

Many times since then I have thought that my interpretation of what I heard was a little distorted, in my zeal to heal the world I took the words to be directed at the world, to be directed outwards. They should as I now know have been directed inwards, I should have made the interpretation from 'Soul Listening' to 'listen to your Soul,' but I am a slow learner. I very often pass the same signpost on my route in a state of shocked disbelief that I am back at the same place confronted by the same old indicators. Now I truly understand what

Soul Listening

'go with the flow means' for when the Soul Listening that I thought and dearly hoped I would be doing for other's, evaporated before me, I accepted it with more grace than I had accepted my disappointments to date. I had 'taken in' the words Soul Listening and I continued to go with them. I had no idea what they meant but I went along with them, and when what I mistakenly thought was a message to give out was obviously not wanted, I brought the message home with me. Instead of putting the words out where they were not wanted I took them in, accepted them and began to go along with them, 'going with the flow' wherever that concept would be taking me.

Me and Soul Listening have been flowing along together since that day. Sometimes we have lost sight of each other; at these times I do not frantically search, I try to keep calm and to go with the not-going. We always find each other again and then, as with any conditioning, my belief is strengthened. My Soul is easier to catch up with the next time we are parted, though now I spend most of the time knowing that we are together, part of the same being. As long as I acknowledge this particular flow (Soul Listening) I am able to go along contentedly without any outward signs of the existence of my Soul (those being its ability to heal and enlighten.) After those quiet times something always happens to amaze me; some-one is sent to me or I make a huge leap on the trail of discovery that I know is leading to the true potential of Me. It happens every time, the flow never ceases as long as I trust enough to ride the rapids and bide my time in the still pools.

But to return to the bit about being heard, or in my case not heard. When I first realised I was not heard I got a little cross about it and in a completely wrong way, but the only way I could see at the time, I set about trying to make myself heard. It was a total disaster naturally as no-one had ever taught me how to do it. That caused me some frustration, I thought I had uncovered the problem, thought I had heard what my Soul was telling me, but it didn't work. It took more Soul Listening to realise that the reason I could not get others to listen to me was because I could not listen to myself. I was putting out again instead of taking in. No-one makes things better for us, we have to do that for ourselves. We cannot make others better but we can make ourselves better. The people who I had been shouting at because they were not listening to me were in fact doing me the greatest favour of all. They were my mirror; they were helping to make a life picture for me to learn from, if I wanted to look. Why were they not listening to me? I had to listen to my Soul and enlist the enlightenment it offered. Remember, I listened by 'seeing' the light of Unconditional Love shining on my problem; then I saw it. I WAS NOT LISTENING TO MYSELF. No-one else could put that right for me could they? Impossible; how could any one other than myself make me listen to Me? It was at that moment that I really knew what Soul Listening meant. I had peeled away many layers of that particular onion to discover the deeper meaning of those proffered words; no wonder I couldn't sing, at the very deepest level I had no voice. I had never listened to myself and in doing that I had denied 'Me' a voice.

There has been another gap in my story, a small one this time, but a space, a break which I did not see coming. In fact quite the opposite of breaking was happening, for when I was last speaking to you I found a flow of words that I simply couldn't keep up with. Instead of the hour that I promised to take each day, I had to drag myself away from here after two or three. It was the clock of duty that stopped me each day when I would dearly have loved to tap myself dry. I know that I resented these intrusions. Time and duties were annoying me, I wanted to shake them off, be rid of the tedious ties of my life and the inevitability of the passing hours. I was making plans, tapping away here; I thought that I was glimpsing the end and I was gaining confidence in the way things were progressing with this story, my journey. Although I never know where I will be taken each day I sit here I thought that finally I could see where this was all leading. I got excited, I could see a nice (here I hear again the wince of my head-mistress, nice was a forbidden word in her English lessons) rounding up, a gathering of threads, a bit of a punch at the end, something to make the previous rambling pages slot together in mind boggling cohesion. It was going to be OK after all. I could even hear the intake of your breath as you gasped applause at the final chapter.

    I made plans; this was to be the final crack at this project. In fact I was imagining much, much more than a project, more than the cathartic exercise I have from the beginning suspected it to be, more than me proving to myself that at last I can see one of my ideas through to a conclusion, more than doing something for myself against all the odds (and there are always plenty of those.) This was going to be something of real value for other people as well. The words that were to take me to a state of self worth were pouring forth in multitudes, so thick and fast I was having real trouble catching up with them. I briefly considered getting out that dictaphone, (at least that would keep pace with the words) but there has been so much that has happened here, using this technology that I previously spurned, that it felt wrong to change transport. I curtailed my impatience and trusted that I was not stemming the tide, that whatever was to be tapped would still be waiting for a voice when I returned to it the next day.

    Even the events of daily life looked encouraging; I patted myself on the back, cautiously of course, I was 'going with the flow' and the result of this was that the flow was flowing in my favour which is what the books tell us,

Soul Listening

don't they? For the first time since my first child was born, thirty four years this July, I was going to be child free; at the same time my daughter is off on a sunshine holiday and my twelve year old is off to the snow. I couldn't quite envisage the freedom of such a situation, one I have never experienced, I only knew it felt so good I thought I would soar. I started to think of visiting all the friends I never get to stay with; this was surely going to be a week in heaven. Then I remembered the dog, the cat and the boy's chickens, how stupid of me to plan for freedom. At the same time I was having my visions of the ending of this, and as I said was feeling cheated each day when I had to stop in full tap; so I made a new plan. I would spend the week here and this time tap till I dropped. I guessed that I would come to the end fairly quickly and then planned to wrap myself up, warm and comfortable to have a read. This would be followed by days of spelling corrections, highlighting, organising etc., etc. to obtain a manuscript fit to offer to publishers. Imagination is a fine thing; it has kept me going for years!

But, yes, although you may never read this, it will be finished and it will be submitted for scrutiny; it has to be, for Me, for my process of coming into being, for a move toward the balance that I search for with my Soul in my mind, and for you. I think I have been offered something that is meant to be shared. It was given to me to take or reject, there has always been choice. Now I simply want to share what I have discovered and offer that to you, then it will be yours as it was mine, to accept and pursue, or to reject.

So there I was, in my imagination way ahead of myself. Reality, as it does, bought me back to base. Foot and Mouth. Having been a farmer, having always had an inner connection with nature, the earth, etc., I could easily go off on a tangent and climb on my political soap-box now. I have done this many times in the past only to prove to myself that, in the larger picture, I am a useless speck of humanity, utterly powerless to change any of the many things which I perceive as completely destructive and abhorrent. I have depressed myself many, many times, both by looking at the situations wrought by man's collective greed (our blind drive for materialism and profits) and in knowing that the only way I can overcome my misery is to close my mind and my eyes to what I see. In doing this I have really given up, it is a cop-out, by refusing their existence for my own comfort I am consenting to the things I deplore. I feel that I am condoning them, hence the depression. Once again I deny the reality, the truth of my own better nature, I shut out the voice of my Soul, which shouts so loudly to tell me that the things I 'go along' with are not right for Me (I guess for many of you also.) My negatively conditioned mind in fear gets the last word, but this word is not in harmonious balance with those words of my Soul, there has been no agreed compromise, one has given way in the face of overwhelming pressure from the other. This is a climbdown, one wins, the other loses. No balance has been found, no harmonious solutions agreed. My Soul, the positive, creative, wise, most loving part of the Me that I seek has been hushed. This is depression. Some aspect of Me has been put down and their Shadows, some dark negative thoughts, some ill-advised conditioning created by my brain, like a cloud descends onto my Soul. This darkness like a cloak veils the positive rays of hope which were ascending from my source of Unconditional Love (or pure goodness, or whatever makes you happy to call it.) This is depression. The more shadows that the brain sends to put down the Soul, the darker the clouds that block our vision, the more powerless then the more 'sick' we become.

Yet our Souls never, never stop trying to be heard, never cease in their quest to pour out their innate goodness, to reach the darkness of our negative minds, to enlighten. Never, NEVER; but in the way that I find myself powerless to alter the huge harmful happenings in the world around me, so a Soul, gagged and smothered by sootied mind energies finds it harder and harder to be heard. This, I think, is what has happened in the case of what we know as extreme 'mental illness'. I have witnessed this many times and firmly believe that severe 'mental illness' is actually the negative mind in full command for it is wholly in charge of the being it is ruling, so creating a truly un-balanced mind. The Soul has been totally shut out, the goodness, the power of Unconditional Love, the light, completely obliterated by Shadows (fears from the conditioned learning of many negative experiences in life, and from lives before.) Now it is the Soul that is ill, the Soul that needs some Shadows lifted in order for it to be heard, felt, seen and known, so that Soul and brain can begin to work in harmony to achieve the balance that is the birth-right of every human being. The balance of mind, the balance of 'being' that will allow each of us to find our true ME's.

I managed not to go off at a political tangent, that would definitely have been of the ego-mind; however I feel my Soul took us both somewhere which was not, on the face of it, parallel to Foot and Mouth. I say on the face of it, because one of the interesting things I have discovered is that nothing is as shallow as face value. If you want to look deeper, peel a few skins, there is always another meaning, another reality, another truth, another and another; the more you listen to your Soul the more layers you discover. It's truly exciting this deep learning.

But, to the point, the trip to the snow of Hadrian's Wall (yes they are 'doing Romans' at the moment) is off; my week of that final 'pulling out all the stops', that spurt to the finish line is off and for a time I was off. In fact I was very 'off' when I started this this morning. I had thought that probably I would have to tell you all about that; but no, my Soul had things to say which were not at all the things which flitted through my mind as I was coming to switch on. After I had stilled that mind, with the concentration of operating this machine to rise to the challenge of finding the right buttons fast enough to give you the words I hear, my Soul made the decisions.

Suddenly, now I feel very, very weary, my eyes are sore and my neck aches, most significantly I hear nothing to tap, and I realise that I am staring dumbly at the screen. I listen to my Soul now. I listen by acknowledging how I am feeling. I am feeling tired, and I explore the ways in which my body alerts me to my feelings. Now my shoulders are aching. I feel I want to stop, although my mind wanted to charge on with this, doubtless for egotistical reasons. I can actually feel the battle within my being. I am two parts, my conditioned mind says, "go on, go on, go on while you have a little more time," my body (which I now know responds to the emotions of my Soul) is flagging, it does not want to go on.

I am continuing, only to illustrate the process for you, for as I do this I am becoming worse and worse, the fatigue is making me feel really ill and I am struggling to see the keys. As I tell you that, my fingers are developing paralysis along with my mind. I believe that this is happening because I have denied the voice of my Soul; in this instance purposely to try and give you an understanding of the signs I have learnt to respond to. I have told you that my Soul, a spark of the Universal Soul, is in charge of these proceedings. I made the decision to keep out of the way, to trust completely in the wisdom of that Great Soul, and to be an agent for expression through my Soul: to listen and tap out what I hear, to try to keep out of the way by being 'the way'. It works, if I keep my side of the bargain. At this moment it is such hard work, I cannot describe how bad I feel and how physically difficult it is to continue now, just believe that I speak my truth............. I have to stop now. ....

It was nearly impossible to get back to you today after a week or more absence. I want to try to explain that. Earlier this morning I discovered myself hoovering frantically, scurrying about with my mind full of all the 'absolute must' chores and deeds for the day. It was like soup in there, in my mind, for I really did not want to be doing any of the things that my mind was assuring me that I had to. I went to my 'to do' list, something I have been keeping for a while; I get great pleasure from crossing the done things out, a sort of mark that I have in fact been here and achieved something. To a lesser degree, I am finding that I'm not able to hold as much in my mind as I used to (blamed on advancing years) and sometimes don't do things which are vital. A sense of advancing senility ensues which I do not like.

It seemed so unfair today; where was the time to be what I have set myself to be? A good mother, a good home-maker, a good house-keeper; let alone the time to create gardens, dig in my own, enjoy the country-side and nature with my dog, play the piano, read, finish off countless part begun creative hand crafts, etc. etc. etc. and even more etceteras.

Then there was this book, my perceived purpose at present, the purpose of the last three years of my quest for the meaning of the words that were given to me then. Time; it has always seemed so precious to me, there has never been enough of it, or so it has seemed. The truth is my time has been as short or as long as anyone else's, it has been a gift for me to use as I thought it should be used; you could say another free gift as it comes with no strings attached, no rules or regulations for the use of. If I find I don't have enough, that the things that seem really important to me are left by the wayside, then there is no one at fault but me. Is fault the correct word? Fault denotes blame; I blame myself, but am I really to blame? Is it not more true to say that what I was experiencing was the state of my mind? STATE *condition in which a thing is, mode of existence as determined by circumstances*. I see as usual that my dictionary has shed more light on the subject for me, for undoubtedly my circumstances, (CIRCUMSTANCE *external conditions affecting or that might affect action*) that is my conditioning, has given rise to the problems I have with time.

As I tap this out I become aware (painfully) of hearing the voices of my two eldest, "haven't got time," "can't stop," "not now, later." This is how the ball of generational conditioning keeps rolling. I didn't see that happening, didn't know what had happened to me so didn't know that I was doing exactly the same thing to the next generation; until now, until Soul Listening. Now I see so much, often things that I don't really want to see; but if I stop and give a moment, a tiny, wee, small drip of my life time to the voice of my Soul I know it is for the best. Then I see the things that could do with a bit (or a lot) of improvement; seeing them is 'knowing' them and then I can set about dealing with them. I can step out in front of the rollerball of conditioning and stop it right there.

Something like that snowball of my child-hood, hand crafted in cold, wet, woolly gloves by tiny frozen fingers, rolled tentatively and watched in awe, the rolling game growing the ball to giant proportions until it was too big to handle. I would let go, see the gathering globe career off down the hillside leaving a trail of green glaring in the whiteness. Now with hindsight and that picture vivid in my mind I see that my emotions were riding high at the event, that green trail somehow defiled the purity cast by the snow cover, and though wondrous at the way that little hand ball grew to be a massive, moving missile, there was also a sense of loss. Chasing after it to its final resting place it became something to throw myself on in a glorious cloud of destruction, rather than something to be retrieved and held again.

Soul Listening

But to get back to stopping that conditioning 'ball' with a view to halting its roll through the years; as with the snowball, as it gathers momentum it gathers girth and standing in its path you will undoubtedly be knocked flat, winded, temporarily submerged. When you do struggle to your feet again your ball will have vanished. With the large ball no longer blocking your pathway or your horizons you will feel (after only a short interlude of pain!) good, really good. You may experience euphoria; you will certainly have a clearer view. You will I know 'cause I've done it, and helped others to do it.

Do you see, as I was trying to explain some time ago, how every action, every scene, every single thing that happens in your life is a picture to be looked at and if you want to, to be seen as something with other dimensions to it? It seems to me that there are layers and layers to be peeled back and each time we do that the same picture reveals a new and different part of the story, a little more enlightenment, a further glimpse of how things really might be.

A clear path and enhanced vision is not a permanent situation; the ball in fact is not destroyed. Like that snowball of youth which disintegrates and mingles once more with the white from whence it came, the essence of your ball still exists. It is however, smaller now, you will have inflicted some damage. Be assured of that and keep that firmly in your mind, for when it reappears heading in your direction (as it most definitely will) that thought (the knowledge that your actions are making a difference) will give you the courage, the strength, the trust to once again and hurl yourself in its pathway.

If all this is beginning to sound too much like open warfare, then please remember that these are my experiences and I admit to being a bit of a warrior. It is different for every one. From my own experiences with others I can confidently tell you that your Soul is your guide; when working with your Soul you will only be offered the steps that you are able to make. I learnt this very early on in this 'work' when I (my ego again) so desperately wanted to help a friend. Our session took us straight to the core of her problems. There is always a core, a theme on which every negative aspect hangs. As you knock a few flakes off your particular snowball or peel the layers from your onion, or as I like to think of it (and hope you may come to also) lift the Shadows from your Soul, the repeating patterns of those Shadows lead you closer to that centre. It becomes so fascinating to see what you will discover next that, gradually, you start to look out for the ball, onion or Soul Shadow instead of dreading the next time you are floored, in pain, ill or finding yourself in the gloom of depression.

To the core of my friend's problems; well that went unheeded, unheard by her though it screamed for my attention. The Soul session that day gave what her Soul intended for her, some help and some insights; it gave what my Soul intended for me. A lesson, a big one, for she did not suggest coming

Soul Listening

to see me again, (well not for that purpose) and my conditioned ego took the bashing it was asking for. I began to learn that the role I play is one of teaching people to help themselves, for this is what Soul Listening is all about, helping yourself.

My lesson was put to the test when people, having crawled along to see me then positively bounced off again; when I was given words like "you have given me back my trust." I had to reject the usual handle applied to such 'happenings', I never wanted to make any claim for having healing powers but maybe I could 'teach' my new belief. My truth is that we CAN heal ourselves. By using the energy of Unconditional Love you can heal you, I can heal me; this is the wonderful truth of the Soul. The Soul is the source of healing; you have one, I have one; ergo, we have our own healing source, and IT IS FREE.

We also have negative conditioning and occasionally I have found it difficult to maintain my position on the 'no-one is a healer' belief especially in the face of huge gratitude and praise. I am a human being who does not yet have a mind that functions consistently in perfect harmonic balance of Soul energy and brain energy; but I shall work on that for as long as I walk the path of this particular life journey.

The learning process is constant if we want it; I believe the pictures that offer us lessons are about us every moment of every day. I also believe that most of us look to be healed rather than looking to heal ourselves. I certainly used to. Wasn't there always a voice in my head (note that comment, in my head) which told me that somewhere was a person who was wise and would be able to help me, some-one who would have all the answers to all those problems I carried with me? Now I know how foolish that was and see how much time I spent on that search, a search I told myself was a spiritual search; but it had to take place. Naturally I did not find what does not exist but I did learn what I had to. I learnt that what I was searching for was not in books or the teachings of others but was within myself. Without that search, which seemed fruitless at the time, I would never have found the gems of wisdom which eventually, when I was able to put them together for myself, led me to the 'healer' I had spent so long looking for.

I now see that I pushed people away and then chastised myself with the thoughts that Soul Listening was rubbish because people were not coming to me. It took a while for me to realise that, even though I would not accept the title of healer, I do have a role and that is to teach what I have discovered and to teach with humility. If it takes longer than I thought then I must not be impatient, I must trust the process as I am trying to encourage you to do. Perhaps the pitfalls I have had and am sharing will pave a surer pathway for you?

Today's pitfall, really my Shadow of last week, was heavily on me as I scrubbed angrily away this morning. You see my head was so full of all sorts of things that I thought I wanted to tell you in this book, I could feel the urgency of it all. So much to say, so little time. Then I looked at my picture, the reflection of my life at that moment. It wasn't easy to look, tears were flooding my eyes, thoughts were crowding my brain, my mind was in a state of confused rebellion and all I could see was my body cleaning the toilet. At such a time why the heck was I hell bent on having such a clean toilet? Was that really priority of the day? Was it truly the thing that the wonderful free gift of time should be spent on? If the answer to either or both of those questions was yes, then why, oh why, was I so dammed miserable?

There was really no need for this question but it's the sort of thing that happens during the time between seeing your snowball, sniffing your onion or feeling your Soul Shadow and making the move to do something about it. This time I have ummed and ahhed for nearly a week, looking at the pictures, feeling the effects of the emotions in my mind and body, knowing the Shadow that has come to be dealt with yet not listening until I see myself toilet cleaning. So I explore the significance of that act. I am trying to make the place, traditionally used for the dumping of bodily waste products, sparkle. I use the word traditional there in full knowledge that the sect who advocate urine as 'the water of life' would not agree with my definition of same liquid as waste, but this belief I think serves to illustrate how varied our own personal truths can be. Anyway, for me this morning it was definitely waste, even filth.

Filth suggested unclean which led to unworthy, then the other line of understanding which linked the waste to the unwanted elements of the food, which is nourishment. Yet nourishment is not just food alone. Now I was really beginning to get somewhere. I have already told you that I was getting somewhat excited by the prospect of completing my story; I (big I) had planned it for this my 'free' week, the week that wasn't to be free after-all. I took that blow very well, now that I am more balanced and trusting in the 'powers that be' that all would be as it is destined to be. So far, so good, until the postman delivers me my book review magazine, 'spiritual' by description. I always thumb through immediately, avidly trying to keep abreast of the new age movement and looking for any mention of Soul. To date, from the things I have checked out which use the word as part of their title, whether linguistically or therapeutically, Soul knowledge seems to have progressed little further than a more general usage of the word rather than a new understanding of what the word truly means. I have told you that I had no idea what it meant three years ago, nor did I even have an interest in finding out, it simply did not occur to me that it may have any significance to life. Should that read, my life? I acknowledge that for many people their religion or cultural background has given them an understanding of the word but for me it was just that, a word.

If I have managed to convey the core Soul Shadow of my existence to you, you will now have an understanding of the feelings that flooded my body and the emotions that bugged my being when on the centre page I find the review of a brilliant new book which to quote 'presents a ground breaking study of the soul and its role in health and healing. It explores.......current scientific evidence for the existence of the soul and its effect on our biology.' I don't blame you if you don't understand the way I was at that moment hit by the largest snowball ever rolled, stung to grief by the most pungent onion ever grown and put down by a Soul Shadow which felt as thick, dark and heavy as any I have felt yet. That was not the end of it, they were my emotions; the pictures were yet to be presented. My daughter shrugged and said "oh well," my big son didn't want to listen, so no sound came forth, and the person I share my life with said "surely you didn't think that the universe was aiming this knowledge at you and you alone? Perhaps you should have been more dedicated; any-one who gets anywhere gets there by perseverance." Every picture pained and with that and my particular core Shadow in place when a supportive follower just smiled and said "perhaps that book is paving your way," I had to stop myself from humphing at her ridiculous (though lovingly given) suggestion.

I had plenty to think about. Sometimes I wonder why I get lost in thought when the quickest way to sort things is to use the Soul Listening technique to heal the troubled mind, but the negative conditioning is a lifetime vessel and as we all know a large ship takes a long time to turn around. I had to think about the various reactions I had had, none of which I received as support; and I had to think about my emotions. I wasn't disappointed, that was not it. I was cross. Yes, of course I knew that Soul knowledge was, is and will be offered to all who want to hear it. I knew it was not mine, so I was cross that it was put to me as something that I hadn't reckoned with. I was cross it was confirmed that I hadn't made it, that someone else with the necessary character and grit of perseverance had published the ground breaking book. I was cross with myself that I had not taught my family to see when I really needed their support. My conditioning swallowed me up, I had failed, yet again, on every count; despite all the promises to myself to make it this time, some-one else had already crossed the finish line. (If you have spotted the punch line here, don't tell me, you remember I am a very slow learner.) I stopped, I couldn't see the point of going on, I felt cheated. I had already caught the odd snippet of ideas and thoughts from various sources which felt like my own ideas and my own words. This had already caused hiccups in my progress; I sometimes found it hard keeping up the belief in myself and in what I was slogging slowly away at getting into words. Now some of those were already there, ahead of me. It was difficult to keep the sense of my value or the worth of this book going.

I did though and this alone is proof of the healing power of Soul Listening. I am here today despite the overwhelming odds that I felt were stacked against me. I am spending valuable time, sitting tapping to produce something which my conditioned mind is telling me is worthless and a complete waste of that precious time. I am sitting here because my Soul has told me otherwise. Its voice, now stronger than the conditioning in my mind has convinced me that the real Me, the Me of the balanced mind, the Me of wholesomeness, the Me of the energy of Unconditional Love, that Me, the true Me wishes to share what it has been discovering. Me believes it has value. Me believes it has worth. Me can now see (as you probably did some lines ago) that although one person has reached a finishing tape, the race (as the analogy dictates) is still going. There are others still moving forward, each in his own manner, making their individual lines to the tape and I am with them, for now I have spent time Soul Listening I know that to finish at all, in whatever position, is to win. To stop because you have not been first past the post is to lose.

I did not know this before. Even though my experiences in life gave me the sense that all was not as well as it could be 'within' me, it is only after the experience of Soul Listening and finding belief in the knowledge that that gives, that I can see that how I functioned before was destroying the potential, true Me. It is only now that I have shared this experience with you that I see clearly the pictures (opportunities) for personal enlightenment that this situation has afforded me; from today's toilet of malnourishment that shows how the Soul feeds me, to the people and things around me who show me the lessons I need all the time. I listen. I let my Soul turn those hurts into healings. Now I feel the joyful surge of enlightenment bubbling up inside me, I thank my Soul, I thank my family and I thank the people who sent me the book review. I'll stop at thanking the toilet though acknowledgement is due; all were signposts on my way for which I am so grateful.

All of which bring to mind the thoughts I had last week when I came to tap to you. I thought I could only sit here and tell you that I had lost my way; my overwhelming emotions were of being completely lost. I really did not know where I was, but when I started to tap, spelling out my acknowledgement of the part my Soul has in this story-telling, something entirely different came forth. As I said earlier, there is a time, and a right time for this process of healing through Soul Listening. It is not dictated by the intellectual mind; it does not work with the ego mind but takes place only with an open mind. An open mind is not something so easily achieved, as I have learnt along the way, but it is worth striving for. Each time I have learnt something I can feel myself smile, it just happens (I can feel it now from the things I have learnt today.) It feels

Soul Listening

so good I forget the gloom of those Soul Shadows, for the truth is that every Shadow is flimsier than the last and when you have dispelled one you can see that quite clearly. For a while each one comes in the guise of the worst one you have ever encountered, but it is a guise, created by the ego of the fearful mind and every time you face that and work through it you get stronger and the next time is easier.

I have got to the point where I can't wait to see what happens next and that sentiment seems a good jumping off point for those chores and duties which no longer loom in my mind as chores or duties. They are just things, parts, components that fit together to form my life as it is now at this moment of time. My life was not always as it is now nor will it always stay as it is (yours neither.) We are linked to the great swell-tide of nature, a constantly changing process. There is so much we have to go along with, so much that is healthier for us if we just move along with it; yet there is so much more that we have the power to alter, to change. This is where Soul Listening can help us achieve greater comfort.

Another day and as I've said I have been sensing that my journey in print is nearly over. I have brought you from there, where my story began, to here, to the today of my life. Arriving here this morning I have had many mixed feelings. The ego, settled today in that part of my mind where some of my previously known negative conditioning (the fearful part of my mind) resides, has been working over time. "Well what's it all about, this book of yours? What are you going to find when you print it off and get to read it? Crap? Who is going to be interested in your life? You've not had much life, nothing that anyone else would want to hear about" and so much more of the put down that my brand of mind has handed me in continual relentless doses. Just when I thought I was getting somewhere. Every time I take a step, each time the inner Me starts to rise, every new peep at the emerging Me that I have been working so hard to discover seems to be eclipsed by that miserable negative mind demon. Once more today I found it very difficult to climb the stairs, a picture which I translate as finding it almost impossible to raise myself; on the deeper level I could have easily allowed Me to be submerged. But the worthy warrior must stand up and be counted, so here I am.

Initially there is nothing to tap out. Intellectually I am in gear, how am I going to finish this? There is nothing in my mind save panic, once again I feel the nothingness of inadequacy, and why is my heart pumping through my ribs and my body shaking? Where is my trust? Then it takes no more than a split second to focus my mind, to use it wisely to speak to my Soul and then I remember the beginning of this, where it all began, before I had even begun to

Soul Listening

learn where the alphabet was hiding on these keys. I remember that some how, as though from beyond me, the screen suddenly displayed that word in capitals, SOUL, and from then on (with the admitted faltering of one who is hacking a new jungle trail with a pen-knife) I knew that my Soul would take us wherever we are destined to travel.

Trust returns, and with it the reminder that I never know where the days tapping will lead, I only know that I will follow as long as the words flow. Now they do not and I am looking at the last word from yesterday, comfort. Strange? No. As I have learnt to see it now, very interesting. I left last time with the word comfort and return to experience myself as it's opposite, most decidedly uncomfortable and at a loss for words. This has always been a dictionary cue. So, COMFORT *consolation, being consoled,* CONSOLE *comfort especially in grief or depression.* I don't know how that seems to you, but to me I feel once again that I have come full circle. I am being told here that your Soul can give you comfort, it offers consolation, at times of grief and depression.

Words...... these words, they seem so inadequate again at this moment. I know that wonderful pictures can be painted with words and have been; but I am so conscious at this moment that because the Soul (what it is, what it means and most importantly what it offers to each one of us) is a new concept to me it seems to require new words in order to put across the ideas in a way that can be understood. After all it is immaterial. It's like talking about God. There has been so much spoken, written, talked about God that we have, each one of us, our own specific understanding of what the word means. That can be very individual and thus very often the 'realities' of the word are so far apart an alien could be forgiven for doubting that we are all talking of the same thing. This is true of most of our words. Our language is used, or for this purpose I should say our language is understood, ONLY in the light of experience. Those experiences are individual and therefor they differ and in consequence our understanding of any word is not universal, it is often unique. In the light of this I am not sure that words can do justice to the Soul, in my truth they cannot, but because at this moment words are all I have to give you, words it must be.

All along this, my journey, I have felt the need to make things clear, to verify the theories, to justify my beliefs; each time this happens the tapping is laborious and my head hurts, it is a struggle to continue and the inadequacy and panic sets in. These are the times to stop and reconnect with my Soul, immediately I have done that all those physical, mental and emotional symptoms disappear, and the enthusiasm returns (I'm probably smiling at the thought) and the flow flows for me to follow. This is how Soul Listening affects me. AFFECT *move, touch [in mind].* The dictionary guides where I intellectually and egotistically cannot! It tells me, for me to tell you, the Soul touches and moves the mind. What is this moving? MOVING *affecting with emotion.* So the Soul touches our minds with emotion. Not our minds touch our minds with emotion, not our brains touch our minds with emotion, not our hearts touch our minds with emotion, but our Souls touch our minds with emotion, EMOTION *instinctive feeling, as opposed to reason.* Soul instinct!

Can we prove emotions are the product of our Souls? I don't know, but my truth is that we know about the various processes of the brain and to date no one has shown how or where the emotional processes take place. There have been coloured brain scans showing areas changing colour during the experience of induced emotions but is this another chicken and egg situation? Are we seeing the brain's reaction to it experiencing emotion and not (as was suggested in the medical journal) a change within the brain which produces the emotion? My experiences with Soul work would suggest the former to be the most likely. In just the same way that changes in brain chemicals and functions have been found in 'mental illness' is this not also a symptom, a reaction to emotions rather than the cause? These chicken and egg hypotheses are circuitous, as is all, and thus I come around to thinking about beginnings and endings and wonder whether the end is the beginning or the beginning is the end.

I began with some words which struck me as very odd at that time, something about Harpic, (which I have never used) and 'round the bend' which to most of us can mean 'mentally ill'. Yesterday as I told you, I was down the toilet again, literally, scouring round the bend in it and I can't help but state the obvious here that this feels a good time to look at these pictures for the further enlightenment which they are undoubtedly offering. I am reminded that I have used the word crap and maybe even shit, (Freud would have leapt in with his perceived significance of all this lavatorial literature; now I want to.) The excreta I have referred to represents matter that our bodies do not want. It has been rejected, expelled, quite simply given the boot and thrown out. It went in as nourishment, necessary food for bodily support or for the gratification of our senses; did the job, served the intended purpose and then anything that could not be assimilated, that is all that was not of any use, came out again. We eat to grow, we eat to maintain, we eat to survive, we eat to experience and our body sorts out from the things that we put into it that which it can make good use of. The rest is waste.

While I am pondering this waste, I am pondering the link between waste in the specific words of shit and crap (and said product getting stuck round the bend causing blockage and ensuing loss of flow) and the waste in in-appropriate nourishment of a developing human being. Does the s and c in us, literally the crap we are 'fed' during our period of so-called nourishment, does that waste from negative conditioning clog within us to disrupt our 'flow'?

Does this type of waste, with no flushing mechanism to disperse it send us 'round the bend'? I believe that personal s and c (in-appropriate 'nourishment' as in negative conditioning) causes all the bodily disorders, diseases and illnesses; the s and c in you and me is learned by our brains and manifests in the body and in the mind. Negative conditioning, fear, excess s and c manifesting in the mind is called 'mental disease'. It is not a disease, it is a symptom (as any conditions that we experience in any other part of our bodies are) a reflection of imbalance.

We all have imbalance of the mind, each and every one of us. In general people do not know balance of mind: if you think you are balanced then you are one of the Angels who some say walk the earth occasionally, although if you have been told that you are an Angel it was most likely in the heat of the moment! Human beings are unbalanced. You and me, we are our minds; without Soul in our minds we do not have balance, hence our continued experiences of dis-ease and dis-order. We have imbalance of mind, thus if we believe this state to denote 'mental illness' then we are all mentally ill! Most of us would deny that, so can we agree that what we are experiencing as beings with unbalanced minds are the symptoms, only, of something else. Could that something else in fact be a disorder, disease or illness of the Soul, shut down as it is all too often by the conditioned fearful Shadows that we put on it?

Can we deny the imbalance of our minds? I certainly recognise mine. Thought of as a piece of string, (as before) at one end mild nervous disorders, occasional panic attacks, alcohol and other dependencies; in the middle a complete breakdown, a stint of anorexia, compulsive disorders and at the other end the full spectrum of serious psychotic disorders. All these and more caused by the s and c of trying experiences in our lives and if you are of such a persuasion (as you know I am) from previous life-times. I don't think I have met anyone who doesn't at some time exhibit one or more of these symptoms of unbalance; you know I've had my share, yet I am usually seen as normal and am confident I would be diagnosed 'sane'. If you believe that we bring anything with us into a new lifetime then we must, surely, have a vehicle for transporting this from one incarnation to the next and for 'holding it' in the interim We are certain that all our 'parts', the physical parts that we know and can see, touch, smell, taste and hear, would decompose and fade before our eyes if we could actually sit and watch the after death process; impossible then for these parts to transport anything. It has to be that immortal part, the Soul, doesn't it; non-physical and as such indefinable? Which thoughts bring mind to mind once more.

We all believe we have one, perhaps you know what it is, you will have an idea, and your understanding of the word will have grown from your experiences. Mine likewise. My understanding, that is my truth, is that the mind is the sum of the energies that drive us. Whether you think of yourself as a physical being or a spiritual being, you are taken forward on your journey through your life by your mind and its energy. The energy you produce to propel you would not move you forward in any way other than physically; with only brain energy you would know no motivation, in no sense of the word, as you understand that, would you go forward. You could say you would not live, you would certainly not 'get a life'.

Can you imagine the life of a person with only spiritual energy? They would not move at all and unless fed and watered on a twenty-four hour care basis would quietly fade away. We are physical and spiritual; we are these two energies manifest in mind. We are powered, empowered and made powerless by our minds.

Mind (the Me and You of any given moment) is the combined energy of brain (memory, cognitive skills, perception, etc., all researched and documented) and Soul: the brain 'driving' the physical, mortal part of the human being and the Soul 'driving' the non- physical, immortal part. We understand our physical energies and witness our brain energies; it is the non-physical energy that poses more of a problem to put into words. In my work I have been calling it Unconditional Love. I have been able to work easily with this for I have my own understanding of it, you could say I know what I mean. The difficulty is that others don't always know what I mean!

Love is not understood by many of us, although most of us have an idea of what we would like it to mean ideally. Because of that ideal, because it is synonymous with all things good, caring and sharing, (some of our perceived 'spiritual' qualities) it feels right to use it when acknowledging the Soul. Unconditional seems to describe the state of that love. UNCONDITIONAL *not subject to conditions,* CONDITIONS *things upon the fulfilment of which depends another.* Once again the guide I have been offered has shown me the answer; having used the energy of the Soul in Soul Listening I learn now that the Soul energy of Unconditional Love needs no fulfilment and has no dependency. It is in itself complete and as I have learnt completeness is a state in which there is all to give. The completeness I have experienced has come at the times when I have found the balance in my mind between the energy of my brain and the energy of my Soul. These times are the ones when I have acknowledged the energy of my Soul, the Unconditional Love energy and used my brain energy to allow that Soul energy to inhabit half of my mind. To me, balance means equal shares, equal rights. I am in my form of a human being, half physical and half non-physical, therefor my mind which is my engine, my propellant, the driver of my human beingness must be balanced by allowing my Soul to share the driver's job fifty-fifty with my brain.

This is where all my problems began, and all yours too; we have not known how our minds work, we have not known what they are. I did not know until very recently that somewhere along the line my mind had become unbalanced; well yes, I suspected, but I did not know how or why, and I certainly had no idea that I could do anything other than accept the way I experienced myself and learn to live with it. Then I heard of the existence of my Soul and I set off on the search for Me. Me being the complete (COMPLETE *having all its parts, entire; having the maximum extent or degree*) human being who is emerging as I train my brain to move over and make room in my mind for fifty percent of its capacity to be Soul energy, pure Unconditional Love. To do that all I have to do is 'clean round the bend', to remove the s and c that my mind has been conditioned to believe in and to fill the gaps with Unconditional Love. That should be true empowerment, and leave my brain clean and uncluttered, in harmony with my Soul in their newly equally shared home I know as my mind. Goodness knows what will become possible and heaven knows what form Me will take then! Me is already more visible than ever before, the balance of my mind is improving, and as the s and c is dispersed my brain has so much more time to work with the energies of Unconditional Love rather than with fear.

Tomorrow I hope I can tell you how my brain and my Soul have been learning to work together while the process of Soul Listening has been unfolding, both within me and with some of those whose Souls have guided them to mine. I do more than hope, I know that I will do this for my Soul has just acknowledged the sharing process and reminded me that it works both ways. My physical being is run by a brain, which so far in this tale has been used mostly to work the machine and thumb the dictionary, now, to get the percentages right, to achieve balance and harmony, now it really is my turn to tell you the practical way of Soul Listening.

Or is it? Can I? I wish that you were here now and could see the muddle that I am getting myself into with this machine. I have scrolled to today's starting point, done something wrong and glancing up have found that I was adding words to the start of this book; then I have managed to separate the text, insert new parts amongst the old, find myself at the beginning again and generally discover that I am completely out of control of this machine. I am in a muddle, going round in circles and making no progress at all with the thing most dear to me at the moment, that is, to get this story and my knowledge of Soul to you all as quickly as I can.

As I try to paint this picture for you, of me sitting here floundering around, I can feel myself with that silly (possibly annoying) grin on my face as the images tell their deeper tales; for isn't the way I have muddled this around

Soul Listening

this morning an exact reflection of Me as I was, at the beginning, pre Soul encounter? Going round in circles, forever meeting myself face to face on that circuitous journey, finding myself back at square one, no matter how hard I worked, no matter how long I tried. No matter what, I always felt that I had only succeeded in taking myself back to the beginning, and from there the only thing to do was to set out again on the same old journey, to cover the same old ground. It was so damn tiring, so confusing, I was drained and muddled, wondering if I would ever get off the starting block of life. I was, of course, actually living, in terms of the days, months and years that were passing I was having my life, but emotionally (remember I now believe emotions are housed in the Soul) I sensed that I was still waiting to begin it. Voicing that view as I hit middle age and more was a real conversation stopper; I'm sure my peers who were planning their retirement wondered whatever I was on about. I could not get going, I could not find satisfaction, some unknown something inside yearned (and that was painful) for life. I said to myself and aloud when I dared, "I'm still waiting to live." LIVE *(being alive) full of power, energy, not obsolete or exhausted.* Aha! There's the answer, I was not alive; that book says so. I felt no power, struggled to find positive energy and was definitely obsolete (in my mind) and exhausted (in my body.) It's no wonder I was utterly convinced that I was still waiting to live. Had I not heard Soul that day when I went looking for the gift of those Soulcards I would still be waiting now. Here and now the tapping process has been slow, if not laborious; another picture to confirm to me, and I hope to illustrate to you, how hampered the way through anything in life, how hampered the way through life itself when we are out of conscious touch with our Souls.

I question exactly what voice I heard that day when I announced in the shop that Soulcards were for Soul Listening, I suspect it was the Universal Soul. No of course there's no way I can prove that, nor do I want to. My purpose is to make you an offering, just as that day three years ago I was made an offering and in the same unconditional way that the choice was left to me, to listen, to learn, to believe, to trust, to test and try or to reject, I leave it to you. I definitely heard the words from without (there is an area around my head, at the right side, a bit behind my ear where things are sometimes said very loud and clear) not within (this area of hearing is the middle rib cage area, where most people place their hands to indicate the home of their Soul.) It seems logical to me that, as I was so out of touch with my Soul within, it would have needed some outside help (a volume boost) to get through my thick skull.

What I really look forward to is clearly hearing, without interruption, the voice of my Soul and knowing definitely that that is what I hear because the s and c voice of my mind is no longer in residence. My mind (the mind of the true Me) with harmonious balance between the power and energy of my brain and the power and energy of my Soul. I believe this is possible. With my Soul now no longer obsolete I am not exhausted; the opposite is true, I begin to have power and powerful energy, according to a most reliable authority, my dictionary, I LIVE. I do, it's the truth. I feel that at last I am walking a line, following a pathway that leads forward. Oh yes, you know, of course I slip back now and then, but I don't fall back very far and I quickly regain my former place ready to head off again. The most important thing is that I know, with absolute certainty, that even if my path is circular the circle is so unimaginably huge that it could take forever to complete it, and what I discover each day of my life now is so enlightening that if I do find myself on the starting block again I shall be raring to set out once more on the great adventure.

That is how it is; working with your Soul is a great adventure. It has its ups and downs, its sun and storms, yet always takes you forward to a better place within yourself. For a long time I stayed within a worse place for myself, I didn't know there was a better one and if someone had told me there was I doubtless would not have believed them. For most of us the knowledge of what we have at any moment is our safety net, however painful, however we are suffering, it always feels safer to stay put with what we know and what we have learned to survive with than to risk a step into the unknown. To do that is true adventure; for those who do not have the pioneering spirit adventure is the last thing on the mind, survival is all. People might have tried to tell me things for my own good but I didn't hear in my surviving only time. We hear when we are ready to act and that time is our own.

When things were so bad for me and within me that the only place to go was even further down, I went there. I was too much of a coward to step off my uncomfortable tread-mill. I couldn't hear you see; though you can see, as I do now, that my Soul came with me; if it had not I would not have survived my personal hell to make it out of there. I also see that everything I have experienced has been the mile-stones and signposts that guided me on my life journey, different ones would have led me somewhere entirely different. They were as personal to me as yours are to you; but however tough they have seemed, in the light of the knowledge that my Soul has shed on those events, I can smile and I do. I am truly thankful and to me that is unbelievably marvellous. I am looking back on times that seemed like journeys through hell and I'm smiling and have a warm glow. Ridiculous but true. That is the place, the state my Soul has brought me to. No regrets, no longings, no bitterness, no anger, no sadness, no resentment, but I won't go on, for if you are like me you won't believe it until you've proved it for yourself; my testimonials won't sway you, you want proof, and I don't blame you at all. So as they used to say in the good old days of Watch with Mother, "are you sitting comfortably children? Then let's begin."

YOU have a SOUL. It is not even necessary at this stage to believe that, the fact that you are reading this and willing to give it a try should tell you that it is coming into your consciousness.

If you want to make contact with someone, especially if that contact is for your well being, (as in friendship, love) or if you are asking for information or medical assistance, it is usual to acknowledge the person you are communicating with. That acknowledgement is made by using their name; to communicate with your Soul for any or all of the above reasons, just open up the channels of dialogue by using its name. "Hi Soul, I'm in the shit, can we talk, I need your help." No reverence needed; no false gestures or ridiculous time wasting regimes, your Soul is there, all ears, forever at the ready, waiting on your beck and call. It is part of you and as such is as familiar with you as you are with yourself (even more so?) It functions only by, through and with Unconditional Love and so, unlike any one else you will ever communicate with it will not make any judgement of you. Be free to talk to it as you will, though possibly in company this is best done in silence for your own protection! You may feel silly talking to nothing, rather like talking to the invisible man; this may not do much to instil confidence.

How to make the Soul real? This is of course impossible in the literal sense, but in the way that we all believe that we have minds, because we experience ourselves using them, so your Soul will become more and more real to you as you use it more and more and experience what happens when you do. At the beginning I needed help and so settled for a symbol which had a physical translation. This has been very useful for me and for others who come in search of their Souls and is a perfect tool for the acknowledgement process. To see my Soul and imbue it with the qualities that I was learning it possessed I decided it had to be a sphere; this being not only the most complete, if not the only complete form we have in our universe, but the strongest form we know. That is the shape of my Soul. Its qualities are everything that you can describe as positive which is epitomised for me by Unconditional Love. So we have a sphere full of Unconditional Love, which needs to get out.

I bought my daughter a present (another present which proved to have more purpose than intended!) She was into josticks and candles at the time and in my friend's craft-shop I spied the perfect candle-holder. Spherical, in simple unglazed stoneware with little decoration other than the shape of some flower-heads engraved around an opening at the top, and a few leaf shapes cut out around the sides: perfect for my taste and my love of nature. My daughter hardly used it and it found its way into one of her drawers, to be hidden in its tissue wrap. When I remembered this I thought it 'made' for the physical representation of the Soul, an ideal Soul symbol, and when a candle was lit inside the Unconditional Love came pouring out; well, the light from the candle did. For me it was an exact representation of what my Soul was doing for me, it was shedding light, pushing up those Soul Shadows for enlightenment.

Now you have the shape of your Soul and can see the light that radiates from it. This is the form to visualise, a ball somewhere in your chest. This is who (if a ball can be a 'who') you will be talking with. In the early stages I did not know that not everyone sees mental images and so are unable to visualise; this caused me consternation as, at that time, the process of Soul Listening was being developed around my own visual abilities. What I learned after I had recovered from the set-back of having two people in quick succession unable to make use of this 'amazing process' for self help and healing was, that you can still know your Soul through sensing it. Had I listened to them better rather than listening to my condition mind which was calling out jibes of ridicule and failure, I would have avoided some suffering, but it was early days and there was so much yet to be learnt. How could I have believed that I was in a superior position, even before I had made many steps along my own healing road, to be leading others along theirs? But as ever the Universal Soul took me in hand and did not lead many to my doorstep, only enough to keep my appetite wetted and to make sure that I continued my own inner journey. Of course that disappointed me at times but I was gaining in power, finding more of Me and going along happily with the things that were not mine to control. The Soul Listening process was definitely not one to control, control being the opposite of Unconditional Love.

So if you don't visualise, you do something else. In the way my 'seeing' things gives me confidence in their existence so your sensing, feeling or knowing will give you confidence; but please forgive me if I continue to describe it my way, for that is all I can do as I have not experienced it your way and so do not know that way. There is no right or wrong way, just yours and mine, each as good as the other, just different; as I said there is no doctrine or dogma to Soul Listening, definitely no rules or regulations, not even a defined format. I never know what is going to happen, nor at my best level of Unconditional Love do I seek to influence what happens; I trust. So now I trust that you will understand the physical form of your Soul and the energy of it and seek to make yourself acquainted with it in your own way.

I am left with a picture of a complete, strong object within me which pours out light. This is what I try to give to those who ask me for help, this picture, or the equivalent. I do this by talking to my Soul and asking for help to link Soul to Soul. I acknowledge that it has the power to do this and just like jump starting a battery the Soul engine purrs to life and the person sitting with me knows (by their own method) that they are in touch with their Souls. As the visual is my own way I admit I am delighted and overjoyed when some-one says "I see it, it's shooting out coloured stars," or "it's sending a beautiful yellow light to me," but these things are not necessary conditions for progress, definitely not.

We are beginning to make contact, and even if you want to tell me, as many have done, that you always knew you had a Soul, this is a slightly new experience for you now. You are making a conscious contact; this conscious effort has a purpose. Until now you have been cruising along with the subconscious knowledge that your Soul will save you, as it does until it's light is completely obliterated and you become temporarily (or often more permanently) ill in body or mind. Even in this state your Soul power will find a chink in its Shadows to shine through; you will probably 'get back on top' for a time, until it gets obliterated again and you find yourself, as I used to, back at square one thinking the adversity overcome only to find it staring me in the face once more.

If you are here with me now, consciously making the effort to contact your Soul, to hear what it can do for you, then I know that you will have ploughed your way through much s and c. You are here because you don't want to do that any longer; you are here because you have an' inkling' somewhere in your being that there must be something better than this, that there must be something you can do about it.

That was the key for me. I had been looking for some-one else to do it for me, and all my searching led me to the realisation that I had to do whatever it was that I thought should be done, for myself. Trouble was that the Me that made up myself at that time was totally incapable of helping itself, that Me had no conscious contact with Soul, even though the unconscious contact not only kept me going but got me out of some pretty horrific scrapes. In touch with your Soul there is so much you can do for yourself. So what can be done and how do you do it?

I don't know what will be achievable in the future. My mind tells me now that with the growth and development of Soul knowledge, with Soul as an accepted and integral part of each human being, the possibilities for our lives and our planet are almost unimaginable; I think that we would not recognise ourselves or the world we live in. That state of bliss though is a long way off.

For now I can only tell you of my discoveries and the things I have experienced the Soul impacting on. In a simplistic statement, it drives away all fear, crudely, it shifts away the shit and crap of our lives, all of it. Experientially it allows an improved state of mental, and following from that, physical wellbeing, by releasing the effects of aforesaid components being 'held' in our minds and bodies. At a deeper level, letting your Soul inhabit more of it's rightful place in your mind means that you function with more Unconditional Love and less fear, you become more positive, less negative, more well, less ill, more joyous, less troubled and this leads to personal power.

This does not mean that you can change things around you to suit yourself. No, the only changes you can expect to make are changes to your inner, then outwardly presented, self. Never kid yourself that you will be able to alter anyone else (however noble your intentions in this direction may be.) However, you can expect change around you. As you alter your balance you will be different, you will react to many scenarios in a different way and this in itself will draw different reactions from those around you, for previous reactions will now be inappropriate. This could make you feel that you are powerful and are changing others. You are not changing anyone, nor have you the right to wish to, remember Svengali; wanting to change others is an ego trip. It is the selfish, lazy option, for we convince ourselves that when others are different then circumstances will be better for us and so we will be different, or at least find it easy to alter ourselves. Wars begin like this, stemming from the belief that someone else is to blame for the situations we find ourselves in. This is a cop-out, the result of powerlessness through lack of Soul Listening.

What you will be doing in your state of Soul Listening will be like giving an invitation to change, setting an example of something different. It is an offering, a picture showing possibilities, but only if others want to look; we all know that you can take a mule to water but you cannot make it drink. You can though take your mule, (the one that is You) and it will drink at the fountain of your Soul because doing that is within your power.

Before you see a lot of change around you, you will certainly find that you no longer view things in the same way. Something like turning a plate over if you never have! It is still the same shape, even the same colour, it feels the same and although you cannot see it you know that it still has the same design on the top side, yet viewed from underneath it is very different. Although you know that it has the same function the picture you now have of it is of something completely new. (If nothing else its shape has reversed!) This is what will happen to many things in your life. Things around you may not radically change but your perception of them undoubtedly will and as this alters so do your reactions and then your actions.

You will find power, it is something you will have to get used to having; the unleashing of Unconditional Love is very powerful in its own very special way. If you are quietly worrying about the abuse of power, in the sense that we normally recognise that word, don't worry, for if you inadvertently misuse this then you will fall flat on your face, most likely in a heap of s and c. Don't worry at all about this either, this is the best mind focuser and you will quickly remember to call on your Soul to get you out of the mess.

Soul Listening

Basically this is what I do. I call on my Soul when I am in a mess. I also count my blessings and give it thanks.

First I acknowledge my Soul by using its name, then I contact it by seeing its form within me, then I ask for help from the energy of Unconditional Love. This is how I do it, but it works just as well however you want to use it. My way has reason and rationality for me, but I know that all roads lead to good. Next I watch for the energy to radiate from my Soul and I direct it to the appropriate place while watching the colour or colours of the beams of healing light energy. It is that simple, nothing to it now, though I did have to take time out and make real efforts in the beginning to get it going. When you are practised you can just make a quick switch over and have a peep at or a chat with your Soul at any time. If the only spare moments you get are when you're on the loo, then that is fine. No ceremony at all needed, after all in reality you are just saying hello to part of yourself. I hope and guess that the process becomes as automatic as the one that clicks our negative mind into action, an involuntary one. I look forward to that day.

That is how I do it, but why and when do I do it?

I do it whenever things are wrong for me. Every time I experience a negative emotion I believe that there is something about my situation that can be improved. I know that a Soul Shadow (that is how I describe negative emotions; the results of negative conditioning resulting from our perceived traumas and dramas of many life times, particularly under the umbrella of fear and the fear of death)) has come into my mind to be lifted. I always experience negative emotions by bodily feelings, and I believe you do too. Anything that affects us, minor injury, major illness, accident, excesses of various life styles, will have an accompanying physical feeling. Hot tears, gripped throat, catching breath, pounding heart, sore skin, weak limbs, painful joints, anything you can imagine. These are the feelings which accompany the negative emotions that affect us, the s and c that we would be best rid of, the fear, the Shadows that lie over the Soul depressing the energy of Unconditional Love and denying You and Me our true potential.

Now all that has to be done is to focus your mind on the negative feelings that you are experiencing in your body and let the Soul shine its beams of light on that feeling, watching the coloured light go to the spot. Concentrating as you will have to, both on where and what your bodily feelings are, and focusing on using the light from your Soul while knowing that that light is the healing energy of Unconditional Love will take every bit of brain power you have, I believe. This leaves space in your mind for the Soul to get in and do its work, for you should in this state have no room in your mind for negative conditioning. Work only on the feelings and with the Soul. If your mind wanders, start over again.

While you watch (or the non-visualizers feel or know) the colours (black and white also) you may get pictures, memories, recollections, knowings, and those who believe this, past life experiences. Can I say a little about this here? I do get these, which means that I believe in reincarnation. This happens to suit me. It feels comfortable. It makes sense of my childhood ponderings. I could never understand how some people, who to me did not seem to be particularly good and certainly didn't look as though they were contributing much to the world or to other people, had long and apparently not too troubled lives, while others, who seemed to be giving and doing so much, were suddenly whisked into the unknown. It also seemed pointless to me to spend a lifetime learning useful things only to take them in solitude with you when you slipped the mortal coil. To state the obvious, reincarnation allows my belief in the immortal, the Soul I am going on about to be real for me. In my 'work' I have found that any past life memories are linked to the Soul Shadows that are uncovered, which tell tales of negative events in previous lives that parallel those of this life.

Whatever you experience, watch it, feel it, follow it, allow it, relive it. Cry (lots of that), howl, sob, swear and beat inanimate objects; anything you intuit to do is clearing the system, cleansing, lifting the Shadows and in doing so, enlightening and empowering you. Do whatever you feel, in privacy everything is acceptable for there it harms no-one. Please remember though that any of the above directed to another, even though in thought, must be transmuted by imagining the Unconditional Love from your Soul flowing freely to them. Writing things down is very helpful, though it can be a bit messy through tears, but do allow yourself to have, to own and to experience anything (however peculiar it seems!) remembering at all times that your Soul is guiding you to be rid of everything that it knows you do not need. You are at all times totally safe.

No-one has ever left here not glowing and with their heads held high, neither have I ended my own inner sessions on a low note. It just does not happen, unlike my experience of psychotherapy and counselling, where on the dot I have been shown the door, often blinded by tears to drive a car home, always feeling ghastly, even though I had started out full of optimism. This has never happened here. Your Soul will NOT take you where you cannot follow or finish happily, healthily and wisely though you may feel knackered after a really big Shadow shifting session, so have a cuppa or your favourite restorative tipple.

The important thing to remember at all times is that this is not an intellectual process; you work only with bodily feelings and your Soul's energy. When things happen just follow through intuitively shining you Soul's light on each picture, memory, feeling etc. Never attempt to work any of this out in an intellectual way. THINKING IS TABOO, at this time. You will be amazed how your experiences will fall into place. Later, (that could be weeks at the beginning) then sooner, your mind will fill you in with all the details and you will understand the relevance of the Soul Shadow that you have cast the light on and dissolved. Your intellectual processes will fill in the details for you. Once you begin to 'see' things and gain new understandings of yourself you will find that you have gained the power to do something about the things that were laying you low. Gradually the fear (the negative conditioning, the s and c) disperses, the power of Soul is in your mind and Unconditional Love starts to fill your being.

Now, be aware. The Big Shadow, your life challenge, more specifically the core of your Soul's mission, will take some getting to; it will have many linked layers and aspects. Don't think that when you have got rid of a Shadow that's it; it isn't. What has happened is that the Shadow is a shade or two lighter, a bit thinner; you have removed a Shadow of THE Shadow. This makes it so much easier now for the light of your Soul to touch you, for you to hear the words of wisdom that it offers. You will be offered the chance to pursue those Shadows, very often, and to begin with quite often you will refuse it. That doesn't matter; when things become too uncomfortable for you you will be spurred into action again. Don't get downhearted when you feel a new one, it is definitely not as thick, dark or heavy as the last, but your negatively conditioned mind, your fearful ego is now fighting for its survival and will be working overtime trying to convince you that you have got nowhere; probably that the whole thing is rubbish and the woman who wrote that book wants shooting. All that is not true and I do give you my word for that.

But I'm not writing a textbook of case histories here so the only testimonials are mine. I thought I was going to say "You will have to trust me;" that of course is a ridiculous and egotistical thing to say as we all look for reason to trust, especially me!

As the word trust is tapped I think of that first day when Soul became something more than a word to me. That happened because somehow it managed to bring with it on those four letters a complete sense of trust and give that to me.

Now I offer the word SOUL to you and I offer my knowledge of my Soul to you and I TRUST.

p.s

My shortcomings in the department of computer skills were glaringly obvious in the first printout of this offering. Hours of spell and grammar checking followed before a read through.

As I searched for the non-existent stories I had believed needed telling some passages flowed and others floundered, some had clarity and others were as 'clear as mud.'

Was the 'flowing' too simplistic? Was the 'floundering' too complex? Was it a mountain of words to sort and sift; a re-write after all that time 'tapping'?

Then out of these thoughts stepped understanding. The energies of the words exactly mirrored the journey; sometimes moving forward, often held back and constantly going round in circles with seeming irrelevance, misunderstanding, revelations, ease, mires, uncertainty, inspiration, hope and healing (and some parts better deleted?)

With that belief and with best wishes I offer all the words given to me to give to you.

Soul Listening

Soul Listening

My thanks to Linda, not just for technical support, but for the most important sustenance of all, consistent encouragement.

note: All definitions taken from the Concise Oxford Dictionary 7th edition, 1983.